Find Your Sweet Spot

Live and Function in Your true Purpose

By
Ian R Peters

©2024. Ian Peters and Citylights Global.
PO Box 654
Big Lake, MN 55309
USA
All Rights Reserved.

Catalog-in-Publication Data is on file with the Library of Congress.

Cover Design: Daniel Peters
Dan Peters Design

Dedication

For my grandchildren, Emma, Evelyn, Charlie, Gianna and Bennett as you navigate the journey of life in this often amazing and sometimes crazy world.

Contents

Acknowledgements

It's been said many times before, but it still bears repeating - no work like this is a solo effort. Many have been involved, and I want to take this opportunity to acknowledge their efforts.

My wife, **Maree** allowed me the space and time to disappear for many hours over nine months to work on this. She was also instrumental in making sure I stayed hydrated and took the occasional break so my joints did not seize up.

My eldest son **Dan**, did a phenomenal job on the cover design. If there is an award for "Book Cover Design," I nominate him. danpetersdesign.com

Eric and **Terri Kruschke** who first presented this opportunity to me and spent many hours discussing ideas till we had a finished product. Check them out at https://www.cornerstonelearning.ie/

Jayme and **Sarah Martin** the Protégés who became the Preceptors when it came to invaluable insights for presenting marketable ideas and pressing me to include more of my personal story to make this idea more relatable. Check them out at beautifulchaoscompanies.com

Everyone who took the time to read the drafts and comment and endorse this work. Your friendship and involvement are my sweetest of relational sweet spots.

All pictures used are royalty free and used by permission from freepik.com. For license information please email the author.

Follow me on:

Website: www. ian-peters.com

Email: citylightsglobal@gmail.com

Facebook –
https://www.facebook.com/ian.peters.583?mibextid=LQQJ4d -

Instagram - @ianrpeters

for daily inspirational quotes, thoughts on leadership, faith and a few shameless photos of my grandkids.

Preface

A few years ago, I began to notice the first stages of what could only be described as burnout. I was doing what I cover in this book. The only problem was I was doing it for everything and everyone that came my way for help. With the counsel of some very trusted advisors and the help of my wife, we decided to take a 3 month sabbatical to refocus and recharge.

The phone was switched to Do-not-disturb, social media was ignored, only family and close friends knew how to contact me, and off we went. The next three months involved resting my body, clearing my mind, doing lots of sightseeing, walking on beaches, watching sunsets, and generally not solving other people's problems.

Toward the end of the sabbatical, I began to think about how to approach the future. My wife had bought me a notebook so I could write down my thoughts. I believe the expectation was that I would have a lot of things in there, so there was something I could sink my teeth into when I got back to work. After three months of rest and reflection, I had only written the following two sentences.

Maybe a big part of this experience is learning to say NO to some things so that the things I say YES to will have a greater impact.

I get the sense that my life may not be as hectic, but what I do will be more intense.

Little did I realize how prophetic those statements would be. I came to the realization that the reason I got to this point in the first place, was because I was not operating in my sweet spot. The result was I was working harder – wearing myself out – yet not achieving the results I was working for.

So, I started to say no to some things and began to focus on the things I felt I was designed for. I soon realized that instead of settling into an easy groove of life and work, I began to be more innovative, and fresh insights and ideas flowed a lot more because I was now operating in my sweet spot.

This volume is the product of more than 40 years in leadership and 25 years of training other leaders. The sections, chapters, and subheadings have been developed by life experience, study, and sometimes, even failures. It's not theory, it works. I know because it has worked for me.

I was first invited to share these thoughts in this format in December of 2023. Thus began the work of gathering years of notes, collating them into a coherent format, and editing…oh, the editing! You now hold in your hands, the culmination of all that work. My hope is that you will benefit from these lessons and not simply gain INFORMATION to help you – as beneficial as that may be. The deeper intent is that you will apply the Personal Challenge at the end of each chapter and realize a TRANSFORMATION as you discover your true purpose and experience the joy and fulfillment of your own SWEET SPOT.

YOU SEE, I DON'T WANT TO TEACH YOU WHAT I KNOW, I WANT TO HELP YOU DISCOVER WHAT YOU KNOW.

Praise for Find Your Sweet Spot

Each and every one of us wants to discover our sweet spot in the world and operate in it successfully. It is a powerful advantage , to be coached into your personal purpose with transcending strategy. Ian Peters has been an imperative coach to us (as business owners)—encouraging us to tap into everything we have inside of us to overcome adversity and succeed in our destiny.

Jayme and Sarah Martin
Founders, Beautiful Chaos®
Design, Construction, and Coaching

Ian Peters' book is an excellent resource that leaders would do well to have in their book collection, and to invest in copies for each person on their team. I know that I will be incorporating the principles of this book into my training and coaching sessions as I work with professionals at all stages of their career and will be including a copy of this book as an integral part of my coaching sessions going forward.

Terri Kruschke, Corporate Trainer and Business Coach
Cornerstone Learning, Cork, Ireland
www.cornerstonelearning.ie

Ian Peters is a simple man with a big heart to bring many others to where they can discover their own sweet spot and purpose in life. I know this book will help you understand what that means and show you how to do it. He has helped me and my husband over the last decade.

Valencia Yip National Athlete,
Kickboxing Champion World Cup Gold Medalist
Kickboxing Federation of Singapore

I love this book - the concept of leaders operating from their sweet spots is truly a unique perspective. This book is well presented, and inspirational for anyone wishing to handle the demands of leadership or to enhance their personal leadership style. It provokes the reader to dig deep into substance. The personal challenges at the end of each chapter are deeply inspirational and innovative – it gives pause and entices the reader to take action. I found the book refreshing and, in my view, there is something there for every reader.

Marie Chin
Commercial Management Professional with a global MNC IT Consultancy

Find Your Sweet Spot, offers readers an insightful guide to discovering their true passion. This book provides actionable strategies for aligning your strengths with your life's work, empowering you to thrive both professionally and personally. It is a must-read for anyone seeking fulfillment, balance, and success in today's fast-paced world.

Thomas G. Fox
Managing Director WaterStreet Research Partners - an Institutional Research Firm

An inspiring journey that beautifully illuminates the path to living your true purpose. With a deep emphasis on faith and seeking wisdom, this book empowers you to discover your passions and embrace them fully. A must-read for anyone on the quest for fulfillment!

Jenny Giese - Business Owner (Fruitful Beginnings)

This book is a master class in leadership for anyone who longs to leave this world permanently changed. Though succinctly written, each chapter has enough depth to be a book in and of itself. That is the experience when one is in the presence of a master.

Lieutenant Colonel Tenay Benes
United States Army (Retired)

I believe this book will save readers years of searching, longing, and wondering about their purpose and direction. Having invested decades in personal growth and coaching, I can confidently say this profound wisdom stands above all. I wholeheartedly recommend this book, and Ian as a coach. to anyone seeking clarity and direction in their lives. This is a resource I would like to add to my coaching repertoire for my clients, and I only wish I had discovered it sooner.

Dr. Angela Bennett
CEO and Founder of AngieB Transformations

Ian's teaching stood out to me for being rational, objective yet compassionate and most importantly Godly. Through his teaching and wise counsel, I was able to find my sweet spot and to work on it to take me higher. Ian's teachings lifted me from a very dark place back up into the Light. Highly recommended literature and counsel.

Jason Lim
President of Kickboxing Federation of Singapore
Director for Active Red, Active Life Center, Active Zone

Ian Peters has been a mentor in my life for over 20 years, offering invaluable wisdom and timely guidance. In his new book, Find Your Sweet Spot, he distills lessons from his rich experience as a leader, entrepreneur, and speaker into an engaging and thought-provoking read. I highly recommend this book to any leaders, whether just starting out or already established, who are looking for personal and professional transformation.

Eric Kruschke

Ian Peters has written a much-needed book in these days when "stress and burnout" are rising. The detailed and practical points will help a person find his/her personal sweet spot and become fulfilled and successful without the stress."

Robert Lum
Senior Pastor, Eternal Life Assembly Singapore
Vice-Chairman, Global Leadership Summit Singapore

"The two most important days of your life are the day you were born and the day you find out why."

Mark Twain

Author

Introduction

Sweet spot - the point at which everything works together for the best results, or most satisfying experience in a variety of applications.[1]

In the world of sports, whether it be baseball, tennis, or cricket, athletes understand the significance of the sweet spot—a focal point where timing, precision, and execution converge to produce optimal results. It is the point of contact where the bat meets the ball in an efficient harmony of motion and accuracy. The result is maximum control and power, propelling the athlete towards success and victory.

In life, the sweet spot is the most favorable convergence of several factors. It involves aligning actions, values, priorities, passions, and dreams with realities. Living in the sweet spot entails encouraging relationships, experiences, and memories that nourish the soul and enrich the human experience.

In leadership and work productivity, the concept of the sweet spot embodies the delicate balance between effort and ease, discipline and flexibility, and ambition and contentment. It is the place where intention merges with action, and where vision meets execution.

For leaders, the sweet spot lies in the ability to inspire, empower, and guide others towards a shared purpose. It requires a recognition of specific strengths, motivations, and aspirations. Leaders who operate from this sweet spot are much more effective in achieving good results. Team members are empowered to unleash their full potential and contribute to the collective success. Productivity in the

---

[1] "Sweet spot." Merriam-Webster.com Dictionary, Merriam-Webster, https//www.merriam-webster.com/dictionary/sweet%20spot.

sweet spot is not about working harder or longer but about leveraging strengths and embracing opportunities for growth and development.

It is essential to recognize that the pursuit of expertise is not solely governed by economic considerations. Cultural priorities, societal norms, and individual values also play a significant role in shaping the landscape of the individual and the modern workplace. Despite the economic incentives for acquiring specialized skills, studies have shown that a sizable portion of the workforce operates outside their area of capability.[2]

According to a Gallup study released in 2023[3], only 23% of employees worldwide are engaged in work that fully utilizes their strengths and expertise. This discrepancy between theory and real-world practice highlights the complex interplay between passion, skills, values, and opportunities in shaping career trajectories and job satisfaction.

One factor contributing to this disparity is the cultural emphasis on improving weaknesses rather than leveraging strengths. From an early age, people are often encouraged to focus on addressing areas of deficiency rather than nurturing their natural strengths, talents, and interests. This mindset persists into adulthood and can influence career choices, professional development, and organizational dynamics.

In many workplaces, there is a prevailing expectation that employees should strive to be well-rounded and proficient in a wide range of skills to maintain their employability. This pressure to conform to a one-size-fits-all approach can stifle creativity,

---

[2] World Economic Forum. (2020). The Future of Jobs Report 2020. Retrieved from https://www.weforum.org/reports/the-future-of-jobs-report-2020.
[3] https//www.gallup.com/workplace/349484/state-of-the-global-workplace-2022-report.aspx

innovation, and job satisfaction, often leading to disengagement and burnout in the workforce.

The emphasis on remedying weaknesses rather than capitalizing on strengths can result in a mismatch between a person's skills and job roles. Employees may find themselves in positions that do not align with their expertise, leading to frustration, dissatisfaction, and underperformance.

To address these challenges and maximize the potential of the workforce, organizations must adopt a more integrated approach to talent management and employee growth. This includes recognizing and valuing the diverse strengths and expertise that individuals bring to the table, as well as providing opportunities for growth and specialization.

Organizations can benefit from presenting opportunities for continuous learning where employees are encouraged to identify and leverage their strengths to achieve personal and organizational goals. By investing in employee coaching, mentorship programs, and purpose assessments, organizations can empower their workforce to thrive in roles that align with their purpose and passions – their sweet spot. Everyone can achieve greater productivity, innovation, and job satisfaction in the ever-evolving landscape of modern life and the workplace.

Ultimately, finding, working, and living in your sweet spot will help you overcome limitations, offering a functional framework for excellence and fulfillment. Whether on the field of play, in the boardroom, or in the tapestry of everyday life, embracing the principles of the sweet spot empowers you to unlock your full potential, pursue your highest aspirations, and live a life of passion, significance, and purpose.

Section 1

Points of
Intersection

At one point in my teens, I decided to try my hand at tennis. My parents purchased a cheap racquet, and on to the courts, I ventured with my friends. We knew the rules from watching the Australian Open and Wimbledon. How hard could it be? The players on TV made it look so effortless. I had even rehearsed my best John McEnroe impersonation - "You cannot be serious!"

First time on the court, I tossed the ball in the air, sure I was about to serve an ace. Swing and a miss! Many attempts later, my opponent looked bored. I'm sure if we had smartphones in those days, he may have been playing Candy Crush while I worked on my hand/eye coordination.

After a while, I began to connect with the ball - though not with a lot of skill. Now and again, the ball would find the sweet spot on the racquet, and the ball would fly. It was not always in the direction I wanted it to go, but as time went on, I learned what the sweet spot felt like and did my best to repeat it.

As I learned more about the gameplay and the mechanics of the equipment, I began to appreciate how I needed to refine my skills. Hand eye coordination and strength were only part of what went into being a good player. I needed to learn to use the sweet spot of the racquet.

First, the frame of the racquet needed to be in proper alignment. It was in this frame that the strings were run in two directions. If they ran parallel or too far apart, it was all but useless. It was the intersection of these strings and the correct tension that gave the playing surface of the racquet its power, each point of intersection adding strength and support to surrounding points of intersection and defining the sweet spot.

If one string broke, it redefined the sweet spot and the effectiveness of my stroke. The further away from this spot that I struck the ball, the less power and control I had, and had to work much harder to produce the desired result.

Using the racquet as an illustration, each string represents a characteristic of our lives. When intersecting with other characteristics we possess and anchored in the framework of our life purpose they provide strength. When we find enough of these intersections, we are well on our way to define and discover our sweet spot.

"Efforts and courage are not enough without purpose and direction."

John F Kennedy
35th President, USA

CHAPTER 1
Purpose and Ability

I was born in Calcutta (now known as Kolkata), India, the eldest of four boys. We lived in a one-room apartment till I was almost 12 years old. Despite our meager living space, we were considered middle class and certainly a lot better off than the dozen us, or so people that slept on the landing in our apartment block each night. Before our family moved to Australia, we never went much more than 3 miles from our home. If you could walk or take a rickshaw, we would go.

If you had asked me back then, I would never have guessed I would be traveling the world, speaking to leaders, and bringing people into a place of realizing their greater potential. My first time on an airplane was when we moved from India to Australia. I never realized that the intersection of my purpose and latent abilities would mean that I would be getting on planes over and over as I worked in my sweet spot.

When examining the characteristics of purpose and ability, it becomes evident that they are interconnected and can reinforce each other to form a sweet spot where you thrive. These qualities are intrinsically linked, shaping the trajectory of your life. Let's explore how these characteristics intersect and strengthen one another.

A Guiding Light

A sense of purpose provides a guiding light - a North Star that defines your choices and actions. It is crucial as it helps shape direction, motivation, and a feeling of fulfillment. - a reason for being. Defining these things helps prioritize goals, make informed decisions, and overcome challenges. An understanding of your purpose also enables meaningful connections with others and contributes to a sense of belonging. At the end of the day, it brings clarity and meaning, guiding you towards a more intentional and satisfying life.

When aligned with your abilities, it becomes a powerful force propelling you towards success. This combination forms an effective harness, leading to a greater impact and satisfaction in your endeavors. Consider your abilities as tools in a toolbox; they equip you to deal with situations on the journey towards discovering your sweet spot. For instance, if your purpose involves helping others, your empathetic abilities and communication skills become crucial. Your purpose acts as a compass, indicating the direction, while your abilities serve as the means to traverse the path.

Dr. Paul Farmer, renowned physician, and anthropologist is a fitting example of a person for whom purpose intersected with abilities. Farmer co-founded Partners in Health (PIH), an organization dedicated to providing high-quality healthcare to impoverished communities around the world. [4]

Farmer's purpose was to address health disparities and provide medical care to the poorest and most vulnerable populations. He was deeply motivated by a commitment to social justice and the belief that everyone deserves access to healthcare.

His abilities as a highly skilled physician and a scholar of medical anthropology enabled him to diagnose, treat, and understand the broader social and cultural factors affecting health. He was able to couple medical expertise with his understanding of the social components of healthcare, allowing him to implement effective treatments in resource-poor settings.

---

[4] https//www.pih.org/paul

In his work with PIH, Farmer's purpose of improving global health and his abilities as a medical professional and researcher intersected, leading to significant advancements in the treatment of diseases like tuberculosis and HIV/AIDS in underserved areas. His career exemplifies how aligning one's purpose with their abilities can lead to impactful and meaningful work.

Discovering your purpose can unveil latent talents and capacities by pushing you to explore new areas and step outside of your comfort zone. As you delve into what truly drives you, you may unearth dormant abilities that intersect with your aspirations, propelling you toward greater achievements than you once thought possible.

The same may be said of discovering new abilities. They may stir hidden passions that bring a fresh sense of purpose into focus or provide added scope to what you already know. As you explore and develop new skills, you may uncover what genuinely excites and motivates you.

It is important that you do not force the issue. Look for what feels natural. Yes, effort is required to improve and excel. Usain Bolt did not become the fastest runner in the world because he simply liked sprinting. He trained hard to improve what was already there.

As a teen on that tennis court, I soon discovered I would never be a tennis superstar. While I had a lot of fun with my friends, I was cut out for something else, and I needed to discover what that was.

This reciprocal relationship between purpose and abilities will increase your personal growth and sense of fulfillment by revealing characteristics previously unrecognized. For instance, learning to write computer code might reveal a passion for problem-solving and innovation, steering you toward a career in technology. As abilities grow, so does the understanding of how to apply them meaningfully, leading to a more fulfilling and purpose-conscious life.

Dealing with Dissonance

But what if there is a dissonance between the two? Typically, this may manifest as frustration or a lack of fulfillment.[5]

Dealing with dissonance between your purpose and abilities involves a reflective and strategic approach to find your sweet spot, where purpose and abilities converge. Start by honestly assessing your strengths and weaknesses. Identify areas where your abilities need improvement and seek training or mentorship to bridge the gap.

Simultaneously, refine your understanding of your purpose, ensuring it is clear and able to accommodate growth and change. Engage in activities that align with your purpose, even if your skills are not fully developed, as this experience can enhance both competence and clarity. Seek feedback and be open to adjustments, recognizing that the journey to realize the intersection of your purpose and abilities is a dynamic one.

Recognizing the intersection between your purpose and abilities is key to achieving your sweet spot and nurturing a fulfilling life journey. Regular introspection and training ensure that you are equipped to live authentically. Your purpose becomes your compass and guides your abilities on the expedition of personal and professional achievement. We will look at steps you can take to discover your purpose in a later chapter.

---

[5] In 1956, social psychologist, Leon Festinger, postulated the theory of cognitive dissonance which posits that having inconsistencies in your beliefs and actual life causes "uncomfortable psychological tension." Psychology. Big Ideas Simply Explained. ©2012 Dorling Kindersly Limited DK, a Division of Penguin Random House LLC.

Personal Challenge

Finding your purpose in life is a deeply personal journey that often requires reflection, exploration, and self-discovery. Here are three steps that can help guide you:

1. Reflection and Awareness
   a. Identify Your Values. Reflect on what truly matters to you. What principles or ideals guide your decisions? Your values are often at the core of your purpose.
   b. Assess Your Strengths and Passions. Think about what you are naturally good at and what you enjoy doing. These often provide clues to your purpose.
   c. Consider Your Impact. Ask yourself how you want to contribute to the world. What difference do you want to make? This can help you align your purpose with something greater than yourself.
2. Explore and Experiment
   a. Try New Things: Don't be afraid to explore different interests, hobbies, or careers. Sometimes, you find your purpose in unexpected places.
   b. Seek Feedback: Engage with others and seek their input on the impact you have on them. This external perspective can reveal aspects of your purpose you might not see yourself.
   c. Evaluate Experiences: Pay attention to experiences that feel particularly fulfilling or meaningful. These can be strong indicators of your purpose.

3. Set Goals and Take Action
    a. Define Clear Objectives: Once you have a sense of your purpose, set specific, actionable goals that align with it. More on this in a later chapter. This gives you a roadmap to follow.
    b. Commit to Continuous Growth: Your purpose may evolve over time, so stay open to learning and adapting. Regularly revisit and refine your goals as you grow.
    c. Make It a Habit: Integrate actions that align with your purpose into your daily life. This helps to solidify your purpose as part of your identity.

These steps can help you move closer to a clearer understanding of your life's purpose, but remember that it is a journey that may take time and patience.

"Knowing others is intelligence; knowing yourself is true wisdom. Mastering others is strength; mastering yourself is true power."

Lao Tzu

Chinese Philosopher

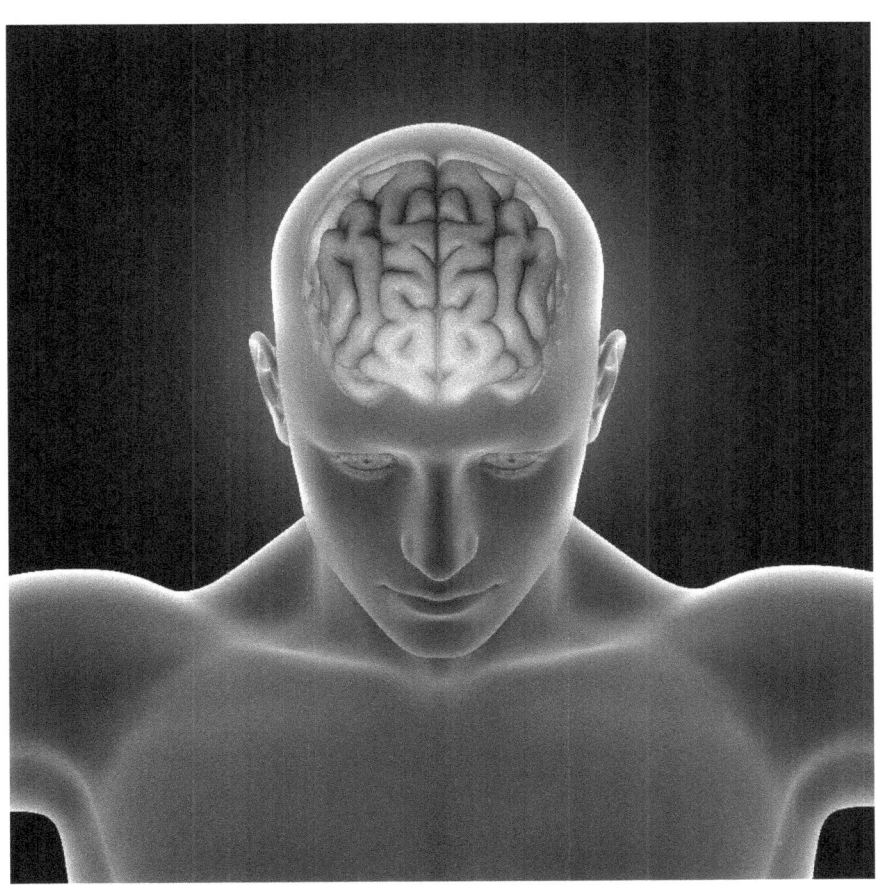

CHAPTER 2
Wisdom and Strength

My first job was in a department store selling electronics. I worked there for about a year to save up for college. Video games were a very new concept in those days, and I remember one particular man coming in with an obviously used video game that he said was purchased about eight months before. He had no receipt and no box but insisted that we give him a refund because he was not satisfied with the game. I should mention the store's motto was "Satisfaction, Guaranteed".

I argued with him for over an hour that we were not obliged to give his money back after eight months of obvious use without a receipt or the original box. Eventually, he walked away, and I thought I had won. A few minutes later, the man appeared with the store manager, who directed me to write him out a refund and give his money back. Even though I had made a correct decision based on the company policy and on the ethics of the situation, I learned a valuable lesson that day.

After the man had left with his $50, the store manager explained to me that some things were not worth the time it took to argue the point. The hour I spent with the man took me away from many potential sales of much higher-priced items. I had the strength of company policy and my logic on my side, but I was not using the wisdom I needed to keep me in the sweet spot of my purpose in that situation – which was to make sales and earn money.

Wisdom and strength are two pillars that, when intertwined, form a robust foundation for dealing with life's complexities. Strength alone may manifest in great fortitude, but the sweet spot of true strength emerges when it intersects with wisdom.

Wisdom

Wisdom, derived from knowledge, experience, and insight, guides our choices and strategies, ensuring that our efforts are purposeful and aligned with our long-term goals. It provides insight to apply solutions effectively and strategically. This application brings discernment to distinguish between situations that require assertiveness and those that may require patience and understanding. Brute force may not always be the optimal solution, but strategic, thoughtful actions often yield more profound results. The product of these two qualities, when applied in the right way, turns raw ability into impactful, purposeful action.

A practical example of the judicious use of wisdom and strength to define your sweet spot could be found in a seasoned teacher transitioning to an educational consultant. The teacher leverages their wisdom, gained from years of classroom experience, to identify systemic issues and effective teaching strategies. They use their strength in communication and mentoring to guide other educators.

By combining these attributes, the teacher finds a new role that maximizes their impact beyond the classroom. Their experience and the resulting wisdom ensure they provide valuable insights, while their strength in communicating and connecting with others allows for effective implementation, defining a new, fulfilling sweet spot where their wisdom and strength align.

Strength

Strengths are the innate talents, skills, and attributes that you possess. Recognizing and leveraging these strengths with wisdom opens doors to opportunities for growth, advancement, and fulfillment. By capitalizing on opportunities that align with your strengths, you can amplify your impact and expand your horizons.

Strength needs to be applied with wisdom to be effective. In life and work, strength alone can lead to misguided efforts, while wisdom without the strength to apply it remains theoretical. Strength encompasses physical endurance, determination, and skill— qualities that drive action and enable us to pursue goals vigorously.

When strength is applied with wisdom, it creates a synergy where informed decisions are executed with potency and determination. This combination maximizes productivity, improves problem-solving, and promotes adaptability in the face of challenges. It ensures that actions are not only forceful but also thoughtful and strategic, leading to sustained success and growth in both personal and professional realms.

Mutual Fortification

Strength fortifies wisdom by providing the confidence to act appropriately in each situation. The courage to make tough decisions and implement wise choices is bolstered by inner strength. In challenging times, physical or emotional strength can be the driving force that empowers you to stay true to your principles as you navigate the complexities of life and work.

Wisdom fortifies strength by providing the insight to act effectively and strategically. It helps recognize the right moments to move, the best methods to employ, and the potential consequences of your endeavors. For example, a wise leader uses their strength in decision-making, not just to act with certainty, but to make informed, thoughtful choices that benefit the organization long-term. Thus, when wisdom and strength work together, raw ability is transformed into impactful, purposeful action.

Correlation

Sound leadership relies on the correlation between wisdom and strength. The most effective leaders blend the sagacity to make informed decisions with the strength to execute them. This synergy is also crucial in personal development, as you learn to balance the intellectual aspects of wisdom with the emotional and physical dimensions of strength.

Nelson Mandela's story is a great illustration of the intersection of strength and wisdom. His strength lay in his determination and leadership abilities, which he demonstrated through his fight against apartheid in South Africa. Despite enduring 27 years of imprisonment, Mandela emerged with the wisdom to pursue reconciliation and peace rather than revenge. This wisdom enabled him to lead South Africa through a peaceful transition to democracy, uniting a divided nation and laying the foundation for a more just society. His ability to combine strength with wisdom made his leadership deeply impactful and enduring.[6]

Conclusion

The proper blending of wisdom and strength enhances your ability to navigate life with dignity and resilience. It transforms strength from a mere display of power into a strategic force guided by insight and understanding. This can result in adopting a harmonious and impactful approach to challenges and opportunities in life.

---

[6] Long Walk to Freedom. Nelson Mandela, ©1993, 1994 Nelson Rolihlahla Mandela. Publishers, Little, Brown and Company

Personal Challenge

Identifying your strengths and applying them with wisdom requires self-awareness, intentionality, and strategic thinking. Here are three ways to do this.

1. Self-Reflection and Feedback

   Take time to reflect on your experiences, achievements, and areas where you naturally excel. Seek feedback from trusted colleagues, mentors, or friends to gain an external perspective on your strengths. Once identified, apply these strengths in situations where they can make the most impact, ensuring that you also consider the broader context and the needs of others.

2. Strengths Assessment Tools

   Use assessment tools like the CliftonStrengths, Myers-Briggs Type Indicator (MBTI), or the VIA Character Strengths Survey to identify your core strengths. After identifying them, apply them wisely by aligning your strengths with your goals, roles, and responsibilities. This ensures that you are leveraging your natural abilities in areas where they can be most effective and meaningful.

3. Intentional Practice

   Regularly practice and refine your strengths by putting them to use in various scenarios. Observe the outcomes and adjust your approach as needed, always considering how your actions align with your values and long-term objectives. Applying strengths with wisdom means knowing when to push forward with them and when to adapt or hold back, depending on the situation.

"Opportunities are usually disguised as hard work so most people don't recognize them."

Ann Landers

Advice Columnist, Ask Ann Landers

CHAPTER 3
Uniqueness and Opportunity

The concept of uniqueness and the potential opportunities it may bring, form a special relationship that shapes personal and professional growth. Uniqueness refers to the qualities and characteristics that set individuals, ideas, and entities apart from the rest. Opportunity, on the other hand, are favorable conditions or situations that can be seized to achieve specific goals or aspirations.

Elon Musk [7] is a unique entrepreneur who maximized his opportunities. Born in South Africa, Musk moved to the United States with the ambition to revolutionize industries. He initially found success with Zip2 and later PayPal, which he co-founded and sold to eBay for $1.5 billion. Rather than resting on his laurels, Musk reinvested his wealth into audacious ventures like SpaceX, Tesla, and SolarCity.

SpaceX aimed to reduce space transportation costs and eventually enable the colonization of Mars. Despite early failures, SpaceX achieved groundbreaking successes, such as the first privately funded spacecraft to reach the International Space Station. Meanwhile, Tesla transformed the automotive industry by proving electric vehicles could be both sustainable and desirable, leading the global shift towards renewable energy.

Standout

Uniqueness can provide individuals and organizations with a competitive edge. In a world saturated with uniformity, standing out becomes a critical factor in capturing attention and creating value. In the business realm, companies that offer unique products or

[7] https://www.britannica.com/money/Elon-Musk

services often dominate the market. Apple's success can be attributed to its distinctive approach to design and technology, which has consistently set it apart from competitors. This uniqueness not only attracts a loyal customer base but also opens new market opportunities that might be inaccessible to more conventional players.

On a personal level, uniqueness in skills, talents, and perspectives can significantly enhance your career prospects. People who bring something different to the table are more likely to be recognized and valued in the marketplace. This recognition often translates into career advancement and the ability to influence needed change within an organization. For example, a software engineer with a unique combination of coding expertise and artistic design skills might be sought after for roles that require both technical proficiency and creative thinking, thus opening doors to niche markets and innovative projects.

Launchpad

In turn, opportunities can provide a launching pad for individuals and organizations to express and develop their uniqueness. When favorable conditions arise, those who are prepared to leverage their unique qualities can achieve remarkable success. The tech boom of the late 20th and early 21st centuries show us how opportunities in the digital landscape allowed unique ideas and talents to flourish. Entrepreneurs like Bill Gates and Steve Jobs capitalized on the burgeoning opportunities in computing and technology, utilizing their distinctive visions to revolutionize industries and alter the course of history.

Opportunities can also serve as a testing ground for unique ideas and innovations. In academia, research grants and funding opportunities enable scholars to pursue unconventional and groundbreaking studies. These studies often challenge existing paradigms and contribute new knowledge to their fields. The discovery of penicillin by Alexander Fleming was a unique finding that, when supported by research opportunities, led to a revolution in medicine and saved countless lives.[8]

Ingenuity thrives at the intersection of uniqueness and opportunity. Innovative ideas often stem from unique perspectives that challenge the status quo and offer innovative solutions to existing problems. When opportunities arise that are conducive to implementing these ideas, it opens the door for innovation on a grand scale. The rise of the internet is a testament to this dynamic. Tim Berners-Lee's unique vision of a decentralized information-sharing system, combined with the opportunity presented by advances in computing technology, led to the creation of the World Wide Web.[9] This innovation has transformed every aspect of modern life, from communication and commerce to education and entertainment.

Seize the Day

The entrepreneurial ecosystem is another domain where the interaction of uniqueness and opportunity is evident. Startups that identify and exploit unique market niches or technical advancements often succeed in disrupting established industries. Companies like Uber and Airbnb capitalized on the opportunity to create unique business models that leveraged existing technologies in new ways, redefining transportation, and hospitality industries. These companies' successes underscore the importance of being attuned to both your uniqueness and the opportunities presented by your circumstances.

---

[8] https://www.nobelprize.org/prizes/medicine/1945/fleming/facts/
[9] https://www.livescience.com/world-wide-web

While the intersection of uniqueness and opportunity can lead to remarkable outcomes, it also presents challenges. Identifying genuine opportunities amidst the noise requires discernment and strategic thinking. Not every unique idea will succeed, and not every opportunity will be beneficial. Balancing the pursuit of uniqueness with practical considerations of each opportunity is crucial to avoid potential pitfalls.

The pressure to be unique can sometimes stifle creativity and lead to inauthentic outcomes. In a highly competitive environment, the quest for recognition might result in superficial or unsustainable innovations. Therefore, nurturing an authentic sense of uniqueness and aligning it with meaningful opportunities is essential for long-term success.

Conclusion

The sweet spot at the intersection of uniqueness and opportunity is a powerful driver of progress and innovation. The challenge lies in recognizing authentic uniqueness while discerning and capitalizing on the right opportunities, ensuring that the synergy of these forces continues to propel us toward new horizons.

By continually reassessing your priorities, refining your skills, and embracing new opportunities, you can expand your sweet spot and chart a course towards ever-greater levels of excellence and fulfillment. Ultimately, the journey towards discovering and maximizing your sweet spot is a dynamic and ongoing process— one that requires self-awareness, adaptability, and a commitment to continual learning and growth. As you cultivate your sweet spot, you unlock your full potential and make meaningful contributions to your own life and the world around you.

Personal Challenge

Identifying unique opportunities requires a keen sense of observation, creativity, and strategic thinking. Here are three key points to help you identify them.

1. Market Gaps and Unmet Needs

    Analyze the current market to identify gaps where customer needs are not being fully met. Look for pain points, inefficiencies, or areas where existing solutions fall short. These gaps can be turned into opportunities by developing innovative products or services that address these unmet needs.

2. Emerging Trends and Technologies

    Stay informed about emerging trends and technological advancements in your industry or related fields. These trends often create new opportunities by disrupting existing markets or opening entirely new ones. By aligning your strategy with these trends early on, you can capitalize on the shift before competitors do.

3. Leveraging Personal Strengths and Resources

    Assess your own unique strengths, skills, and resources that can be leveraged to create a competitive advantage. Opportunities often arise when you can combine your personal assets with a market need or emerging trend in a way that others cannot easily replicate. This could involve tapping into your network, using specialized knowledge, or capitalizing on unique experiences.

"Educating the mind without educating the heart is no education at all."

Aristotle
Greek Philosopher

CHAPTER 4
Intellect and Values

As we have seen so far, finding your sweet spot in life – a state with personal fulfillment, professional success, and meaningful contribution converge – requires a deep understanding of where various characteristics of life intersect. This journey involves navigating the intricate interplay between intellect and values. Intellect, a big part of this, encompasses our cognitive abilities and knowledge. Our values are our core beliefs and principles. Together, they form a significant part of the foundation on which our decisions and actions are based. So, how do these two critical aspects intersect and help us discover our unique sweet spot?

Understanding Intellect and Values

When we think about intellect, we often picture problem-solving, learning, and making decisions. But intellect isn't just about being "smart"—it's how we use what we've picked up from school, experiences, and even mistakes to navigate life. Your intellect helps you understand the world, solve problems, and make informed decisions. It's like a toolkit full of everything you've learned over time, giving you the ability to handle whatever comes your way. However, knowing how to solve problems isn't enough on its own—this is where values come in.

Values are the deeply held beliefs that guide you through life. They come from your upbringing, your culture, your personal experiences, and even your spiritual views. Whether it's honesty, compassion, or ambition, your values are like a compass, directing how you use your intellect to make choices that truly matter to you. In other words, intellect gives you the tools to think through decisions, but values help you decide which decisions to make and how to act in a way that feels right to you.

Take a moment to reflect on your own strengths. Maybe you're good at thinking outside the box or solving problems quickly. Now think about what you value most. Is it integrity? Loyalty? Personal growth? These qualities, when combined, shape not only what you're capable of doing but also how you choose to live your life. They're what make you more than just someone who's skilled at their job—they make you someone with a deeper sense of purpose and direction.

I've personally seen this intersection of intellect and values play out in my own life. For instance, at one point I had to choose between a career path that offered financial security and another that aligned more closely with my passion for helping others. It wasn't an easy decision, but in the end, my values led me to the path that felt more meaningful, even if it wasn't the most lucrative. And I've never regretted it, because aligning my work with my values has given me a sense of purpose that money couldn't replace.

So, how do intellect and values come together to guide your life choices? It's through reflection and balance. Your intellect helps you identify your strengths—what you're good at—and your values help you figure out what really matters. Together, they help you make decisions that not only lead to success but also bring you fulfillment. The key is finding where your intellect and values intersect, so you can live a life that feels both rewarding and true to who you are.

The Role of Intellect

Intellect plays a crucial role in identifying and understanding your strengths and weaknesses. Through study, assessment, and reflection, you can identify your capabilities, and how these can be leveraged to achieve personal and professional goals. For example, a person with strong analytical skills might find fulfillment by applying their prowess in careers that involve problem-solving and strategic planning.

Intellectual curiosity drives you to explore different fields, acquire new knowledge, and develop expertise. This continuous learning process can help you identify areas where you excel and feel passionate, bringing you closer to your sweet spot. It also enables you to set realistic and achievable goals, plan strategically, and adapt to changing circumstances.

However, intellect without values can lead to a disjointed and unsatisfying pursuit of success. It is values that imbue your intellectual endeavors with purpose and meaning.

The Role of Values

Values are essential in guiding you towards activities and goals that resonate with your sense of purpose and fulfillment. While intellect can identify what you are good at, values help determine and prioritize what is worth pursuing. For instance, you may have the intellectual capacity to excel in a high-paying corporate management job but may find true fulfillment in a charitable profession that aligns more with your values, such as running a homeless shelter or social work. Whatever career you choose, the point is to find the place where you align what you know with who you are deep inside.

Another important aspect of identifying your values is that they can act as a motivator, driving you to persevere through challenges and setbacks. When what you do is aligned with deeply held convictions, you are more likely to remain committed and able to find a way to bounce back, even in the face of adversity.

The Intersection of Intellect and Values

With a solid understanding of both intellect and values, the next challenge is discovering where they intersect in your life. This intersection forms the core of your sweet spot, where intellect and values work together to guide your purpose. As such it must become a critical part of defining your sweet spot.

Of all the intersecting lines that help identify your sweet spot, the juncture of these two speaks more about who you are as a person, than about what you do. As such it must become a critical part of defining your sweet spot. This alignment ensures that your talents are used in service of what you believe to be important, creating a harmonious balance between personal satisfaction and meaningful contribution.

That said, let's take a brief look at a part of the process of defining this intersection. Some of these areas will be examined in more detail in later chapters.

1. Reflection. This is not a one-and-done step. As we grow, our abilities and worldview moderates. You will need to engage in deep reflection to understand your cognitive strengths and your core values. Tools, such as personality assessment10, reading, feedback from others, and introspective practices like journaling, and academic and spiritual study can facilitate this process. Understanding yourself fully is the first step towards aligning intellect and values.

2. Identifying Passion. Passion often lies at the intersection of what you love, or are good at, and what you believe in. By exploring the benefits and setbacks of different activities and careers, you can identify where your intellect and values

---

[10] www.16personalities.com

align and how they impact you. It is a quality that is hard to quantify, but we all need passion to guide us through the trials, challenges, and successes of life. See more on this subject in Chapter 16.

3. Setting Goals. When setting goals, it's important to ask yourself not just 'What can I achieve?' but also 'What aligns with my core values?' I've found that the goals that are more aligned with my values are the ones that I am most passionate about pursuing, even when challenges arise.

4. Learning and Adapting. The journey to your sweet spot is not static; it requires continuous learning and adaptation. As you grow and mature, your intellect and values may also adapt. Staying open to new experiences and learning opportunities allows you to refine your understanding and realign your goals accordingly.

5. Create a Personal Mission Statement. A personal mission statement can serve as a guiding star for your decisions and actions. It encapsulates your values, strengths, and aspirations, providing clarity and direction. See Personal Challenge at the end of this chapter on How to Write a Mission Statement.

Education and Advocacy

Malala Yousafzai, [11] the youngest Nobel prize laureate, exemplifies the powerful intersection of intellect and values in her advocacy for girls' education. Despite facing life-threatening adversity, Malala's intellectual capabilities and deep-seated value for education and equality, drove her to become a global symbol of courage and change. Her speeches, writings, and activism are a

---

[11] https://www.womenshistory.org/education-resources/biographies/malala-yousafzai

testament to how aligning intellect with values can lead to profound societal impact and personal fulfillment.

Innovation and Sustainability

Elon Musk,[12] the CEO of X (formerly Twitter), SpaceX, and Tesla, demonstrates how intellect and values intersect to drive revolutionary advancements. Musk's intellectual prowess in engineering and business, combined with his values of sustainability and exploration, has led to significant contributions in space travel, electric vehicles, and renewable energy. Musk's ventures reflect a harmonious blend of his cognitive skills and commitment to creating a sustainable future.

Challenges and Barriers

While the intersection of intellect and values can lead to profound fulfillment, there are challenges and barriers that a person may face. External pressures, fear of failure, internal conflicts, or contribute to boundaries that limit personal achievement.

In many parts of the world, limited access to academic, financial, and social resources can hinder the pursuit of goals that align with your intellect and values. Seeking mentorship, building networks, and leveraging available resources are crucial strategies for overcoming these barriers.

Abraham Lincoln overcame significant challenges, including poverty, limited formal education, and political setbacks.[13] Despite losing multiple elections and facing personal failures, Lincoln's unyielding commitment to his values of equality and justice fueled his resilience. Each setback only sharpened his intellect and

---

[12] https://www.britannica.com/money/Elon-Musk
[13] https://www.history.com/topics/american-civil-war/election-of-1860#section_1

strengthened his resolve, until finally, these trials culminated in his election as President.

He educated himself, worked various jobs, and developed strong oratory skills. Despite losing multiple elections, his perseverance and dedication to abolition and unity eventually led to his election as the 16th President of the United States.

Conclusion

The intersection of intellect and values is a powerful convergence that guides you towards your sweet spot, where personal fulfillment, professional, success, and societal contribution find harmony. By understanding and leveraging your intellectual strengths, and aligning them with deeply held values, you can navigate life's complexities with clarity and live your purpose. Historical and contemporary examples - from Steve Jobs to Malala Yousafzai - illustrate the profound impact of this alignment. Ultimately, finding your sweet spot is a dynamic process that evolves with your growth and experiences, leading to a deeply satisfying and purposeful life.

As you operate within the intersection of purpose, ability, wisdom, strength, uniqueness, and opportunity, you discover a sweet spot—a dynamic space where your endeavors are fueled by passion, guided by insight, and empowered by your innate talents and capabilities. Over time, as you focus more on activities and pursuits that align with your sweet spot, you experience greater fulfillment, effectiveness, and success in your endeavors.

Personal Challenge

Writing a personal mission statement involves clearly defining your purpose, goals, and values. Here's a step-by-step guide:

1. Identify Core Purpose

   What is the fundamental reason for your being? Consider the impact you want to have on your family, community, or work. The core purpose should reflect a broader intention beyond just fame and fortune.

2. Outline Key Goals

   Highlight your primary objectives. These goals should be specific enough to guide decision-making but broad enough to allow for growth and adaptation. Consider what success looks like for you in the long term.

3. Reflect Personal Values

   Include the core values that guide your behavior and decision-making. These values should resonate with your family, friends, and community. They form the ethical foundation of your mission statement, indicating how you intend to achieve your goals.

Example Structure:

"My mission is to [core purpose] *by* [key goals], *while* [your values]."

Example Mission Statement:

"My mission is to empower those in my circle by providing innovative personal, professional, and material benefits, while maintaining a commitment to integrity, sound relationships, and mutual respect."

Keep the statement concise, memorable, and reflective of your unique identity. It should inspire and guide those in direct and indirect relationships with you.

"Synchronicity is an ever-present reality for those who have eyes to see."

Carl Jung

Swiss Psychologist

CHAPTER 5
Synchronicity

Synchronicity[14] is a term coined by Swiss psychologist Carl Jung to describe the phenomena where you become aware of a meaningful connection between two seemingly unrelated events or experiences. Jung's exploration of synchronicity emerged from his deep engagement with the realms of psychology, philosophy, and spirituality, reflecting his belief in the existence of a meaningful order underlying the apparent chaos of life. It was this framework for his study that led him to the understanding that synchronicity transcends the realm of mere coincidence, suggesting a deeper, underlying harmony or significance in the fabric of reality. One such moment of synchronicity in my own life came when I moved from Australia to the USA.

I have been involved in church my whole life. As a teenager in the 70s, I remember attending a conference in Sydney, Australia. At that point, it was the largest church conference in the Southern Hemisphere. Leading that conference was a man named Alan Langstaff. I watched him on the platform, which had some of the highest-profile names in the church world. Along with many thousands of people, I watched and admired his leadership as he led this conference with great poise, yet great humility.

Two decades later, I moved from Australia to the USA. Within a few weeks of my arrival, someone suggested to me that I meet this other Australian that they had come to know. I agreed and walked into the appointment only to see Alan Langstaff there to greet me.

---

[14] Synchronicity. An Acausal Connecting Principle. C G Jung, Translation by R F C Hull. ©1960 Bollingen Foundation, New York, N.Y. Second Edition ©1969 Princeton University Press.

There was a rush of emotions at the unexpected meeting with a hero of mine. During that meeting he shared his experience of moving to the USA with a young family and gave me some much appreciated advice on how to navigate some of my apprehensions. And it came with the added bonus of an Aussie perspective. That was in 2000. What could be described as a chance meeting has turned out to be a relationship of immense value. Since that time, he has not only been a mentor to me, but we have developed a great friendship, and he has opened many doors that has helped me to become the person I am today.

Connections and Their Significance

These connections often occur during times of spiritual or psychological significance, such as periods of transition, crisis, or introspection. In such moments, the boundaries between seemingly unrelated realms fade, allowing for the connection to become more apparent, helping us to realize our sweet spot. While each instance on its own may seem insignificant, when viewed collectively, they create a sense of resonance or importance that often defies rational explanation.

At its core, synchronicity is about recognizing and interpreting meaningful patterns or connections that emerge, sometimes without any apparent link. These connections can manifest in various forms, such as shared themes, symbols, or even parallel occurrences in distinct aspects of life. Unrelated events can sometimes align in surprising, synchronous ways. Some may see these as coincidence or serendipity.

Alexander Fleming's discovery of penicillin in 1928 was one such event that has impacted most people on this planet. He noticed that a mold, later identified as Penicillium notatum, had contaminated his petri dishes and killed surrounding bacteria. This chance observation led to the discovery of penicillin, the world's first antibiotic, revolutionizing medicine by effectively treating bacterial infections and saving countless lives. Fleming's keen observation turned an accidental finding into a tremendous medical breakthrough.[15]

Chemistry

Have you ever experienced a moment where coincidence felt too meaningful to be random? Synchronicity can occur in interpersonal relationships, where one person perceives a profound connection with another, despite the lack of any logical basis for it. Some may call it chemistry. This feeling often arises from shared experiences, values, or beliefs that resonate deeply with each other, leading to a sense of mutual understanding and connection.

Synchronicity highlights the interconnectedness of human perception, suggesting that meaning is not always confined to linear cause-and-effect relationships. Instead, it invites us to embrace the mystery and complexity of our existence, acknowledging that sometimes, the most profound moments of revelation can come through seemingly random or unrelated events.

This chemistry is not always about romantic relationships. Successful business partnerships often arise from chance relationships.

Steve Jobs and Steve Wozniak met through a mutual friend at a casual gathering, eventually co-founding Apple and with significant input from their friend, Ronald Wayne, transformed the tech industry.[16] Similarly, Ben Cohen and Jerry Greenfield reconnected

---

[15] https://www.nobelprize.org/prizes/medicine/1945/fleming/facts/
[16] https://www.macworld.com/article/671584/history-of-apple-the-story-of-steve-jobs-and-the-company-he-founded.html

after high school and founded Ben & Jerry's, one of the most iconic ice cream brands.[17] A fortuitous encounter at a conference led Larry Page and Sergey Brin to co-found Google.[18] Much like my chance encounter with Alan Langstaff, these partnerships reveal how synchronicity can shape the trajectory of a life in ways we can never fully predict.

These examples illustrate the synchronicity of how casual, unexpected encounters can lead to powerful, often profitable, and life-altering collaborations. Stories like this show the importance of networking and openness to new opportunities in the business world. It is important to not over analyze each situation or just to look for people that are useful to your end goal. As you grow in your discovery of your sweet spot, be aware of the intersectional relationships that may come across your path from time to time.

Why it Matters

So, what does all this mean when it comes to helping you find your sweet spot in life?

Whether you believe in fate, coincidence, or the Divine hand of God, there are some aspects of life that defy – or, at best, challenge – explanation or understanding. The concept of synchronicity helps clarify much of this. The beauty of life lived with purpose, is that it comes with a mysterious sense of alignment.

Along with the scientific process of cause and effect, there is a place for acknowledging the sometimes-mysterious role of simply being, and its accompanying symbolism that helps shape our human experience.

---

[17] Ben and Jerry's: The Inside Scoop. ©1994 by Fred Lager. Published by Crown Publishers, Inc.
[18] https://about.google/intl/ALL_us/our-story/

The fact that you are in your situation impacts and shapes your environment and the people around you. You bring something unique to the mix when you interact with others. This is reciprocated in every situation to varying degrees.

Consider the fact that you are reading this right now. Whether by another person's influence, chance, or some other design, it is evoking some type of response in you. If it is a positive response, hopefully, the synchronicity of this moment will help you move toward the realization of your sweet spot. If the feeling is indifferent or negative, that will trigger a corresponding reaction caused by the synchronicity of this event.

Making it Make Sense

In amongst all this, there are some profound implications for our understanding of human existence, and the nature of reality. It suggests that there is an inherent order and intelligence pervading the universe, one that transcends the limitations of linear causality, and our ability to comprehend it.

Finding your sweet spot does not have to be a struggle. Understanding the concept of synchronicity helps remove some of the struggle and dogged determination that many feel necessary to realize their goals in life. Whether viewed as a psychological phenomenon, a spiritual principle, or a fundamental aspect of your existence, understanding synchronicity continues to captivate the human imagination, and inspire avenues of exploration on the journey to finding and living in your sweet spot.

Personal Challenge

Recognizing synchronicity involves tuning in to meaningful coincidences and understanding their potential significance in your life. Here are three key points to help you recognize synchronicity:

1. Heightened Awareness of Patterns and Repetition

   Pay attention to recurring themes, numbers, symbols, or events in your life. These patterns may seem coincidental but can hold a deeper meaning or guide you toward a particular direction or decision.

2. Emotional Resonance and Intuition

   Trust your gut feelings when something stands out or feels unusually significant. If an event or coincidence triggers a strong emotional response or a sense of knowing, it might be a sign of synchronicity that is worth exploring.

3. Alignment with Intentions or Questions

   Notice when events or encounters seem to align perfectly with your current thoughts, questions, or desires. Synchronicities often occur when you are seeking answers or guidance, appearing as if an unseen hand is responding directly to your inner state or intentions.

"Success is not the key to happiness. Happiness is the key to success. If you love what you are doing, you will be successful."

Albert Schweitzer

Humanitarian

CHAPTER 6
How Finding Your Sweet Spot Helps

I was six hours away from getting on a plane to travel to Zambia for a large leadership conference when we got the news that the nation was beginning a lockdown because of COVID-19. Like millions around the planet, I was faced with thoughts about my future, my well being and that of my family, and, not the least on my list of concerns was my income.

The next two years were a frenetic mix of phone calls, video conferences, and dealing with individuals as I coached them on how to navigate this unique situation. I found myself dealing with everything from peoples depression and anxiety, to helping non-profit organizations deal with lack of regular financial support, and small business owners talking to staff about layoffs, all in the hope that "this couldn't last much longer, could it." Because I work with many people in time zones across the globe, many of these calls kept me up at all hours of the night. For someone who is in a different time zone every two or three weeks, you would think that this would be a time of rest. It turns out the exact opposite was the case.

I was operating on fumes - often without the normal income that my work brings. Somehow, we made it financially, but towards the end of 2021, I realized that I had begun to experience the effects of burnout. Through the counsel and help of mentors and peers, my wife and I took a sabbatical. I switched my phone to do-not-disturb, and for the next three months ,our biggest decision was whether to walk along the beach ,read by the pool, or in the air-conditioned comfort off of the recliner. We took a long road trip through some of this nation's great national parks and simply enjoyed the time sightseeing and replenishing body, soul, and spirit.

It was during this time I realized that I was operating outside of my sweet spot, and that became the genesis of this book.

Finding the intersection where purpose and abilities, wisdom and strength, uniqueness and opportunities, and intellect and values align has a profound impact on many aspects of your life. Of course, these are a small sampling of the converging points of your life. The goal is to discover as many as possible and determine how they fit together to define your sweet spot.

Emotional well-being

Despite many personal challenges, I did find myself operating in my sweet spot now and then. In 2015, I reconnected with a couple who were childhood friends from India. Now married to each other, they had a passion to begin a refuge home for victims of human sex trafficking. Even though I have no personal experience in this area, I decided to get on board with their vision. As the girls came through the refuge, they received care, counseling, physical and emotional treatment and above all the sense of belonging to a family.

It soon became clear that this project was desperately in need of a reliable vehicle. A simple task like getting groceries to the home during the COVID lockdowns, became a logistical exercise in negotiating curfews, supply issues and having to hire a car and driver to get the purchases to the girls. We decided a reliable used vehicle would do the trick and began the process of appealing to donors for help. The appeals finally attracted the attention of one individual who had been to India with me 15 years before. Over lunch he heard details of the need and potential resolutions and expressed his opinion that a used vehicle would not do the job. That moment of deflation turned into full blown elation as he wrote a check to cover the purchase of a brand new 8 seater van.

It's hard to describe the emotions during the next Zoom call. Tears of joy, laughter and maybe even a little dancing filled the next few minutes as I explained what had come about. The lines of passion, ability, opportunity intersected in that moment of synchronicity and a significant need was met. Due to the supply issues during that time, it took a while for delivery, but the next time I made the trip to see the girls, I was picked up in a beautiful new van. Not only has this solved many logistical issues of transport, no feeling could compare with watching and listening to the girls showing me their new vehicle.

When you operate within your sweet spot, it brings a feeling of fulfillment and satisfaction. This alignment promotes positive and resilient emotions, nurturing a profound sense of purpose and direction in life. When your actions are in harmony with your core beliefs and desires, you experience greater emotional stability and contentment. You will find yourself better equipped to navigate the complexities of daily life with grace and durability, allowing you to thrive and flourish amidst the ever-changing landscape of human experience.

Emotional well-being is not always about making money or climbing the corporate ladder. I personally know of doctors, nurses, lawyers, and other professionals who discovered the joy of volunteering their expertise in situations where they are not paid or even recognized.

Engaging in rewarding work triggers the release of endorphins, the brain's natural "feel-good" chemicals. These endorphins elevate mood, reduce stress, and enhance overall well-being.[19] When you perform meaningful tasks, the brain rewards you with a sense of pleasure and satisfaction. This biochemical response not only boosts

---

[19] https://www.healthline.com/health/endorphins

happiness but also fosters motivation and strength, creating a positive feedback loop that encourages continued engagement in fulfilling activities.[20]

The impact becomes exponential. Better performance contributes to a better state of mind, which increases performance… and on it goes.

Physical well-being

Likewise, engaging in activities that resonate with your purpose, passions, and strengths impacts your physical health. People who engage in activities about which they are enthusiastic - whether it's hiking in nature or playing a favorite sport - often experience increased levels of endorphins. This, in turn, results in reduced stress levels, pain relief, euphoria, and even an improvement in the immune system, lowering the risk of heart disease, hypertension, and other chronic conditions. Better sleep patterns and increased energy are also healthy byproducts of a fulfilling life.[21]

When you focus on activities that leverage your strengths and abilities, you build new levels of experience and a sense of competence and mastery. This can lead to increased self-confidence and motivation to maintain healthy habits. Whether it's lifting weights, dancing, or participating in team sports, activities that align with your sweet spot will often enhance physical well-being and overall vitality.

---

[20] Endorphins are the body's natural pain relievers and mood boosters. They are naturally produced during pleasurable activities like exercise, sex, and laughing, as well as painful experiences, such as twisting your ankle.
[21] Ryff, C. D., & Singer, B. (2008). Know thyself and become what you are: A eudaimonic approach to psychological well-being. Journal of Happiness Studies, 9, 13-39.

Job Performance

Discovering and leveraging your sweet spot enhances job satisfaction, engagement, and performance. When you can utilize your strengths, pursue meaningful work, and contribute to a larger purpose, you become more motivated, productive, and committed to achieving excellence in your role.

Efficiency and effectiveness are distinct concepts that are often conflated. Efficiency focuses on doing things right. It is entirely possible to do perform a task correctly, but is not always productive because it focuses on doing tasks quickly rather than on achieving meaningful outcomes. Without clear goals or quality standards, efficient processes can lead to poor results and missed opportunities. In all areas of life, true productivity requires balancing speed with effectiveness and aligning efforts with intended objectives.

Effectiveness pertains to doing the right things. It prioritizes selecting and executing tasks that directly contribute to desired, necessary outcomes. This might involve identifying and focusing efforts on high-impact activities while disregarding less consequential tasks. Success hinges on finding the point of intersection between efficiency and effectiveness, ensuring that efforts are not only optimized but also directed toward meaningful goals. For example, a sales rep may make a quarter of the scheduled sales calls each day, but in the end, it's not calls; it's sales that are the goal. Find out why certain calls turn into sales, and you have found a sweet spot.

Return on Investment (ROI)

ROI extends beyond financial metrics; it encompasses the value gained from investing time, energy, and resources into activities that align with personal strengths and passions. When you focus on endeavors that resonate with your sweet spot, you unlock a higher

ROI, experiencing profound personal and professional benefits. For me, securing that van for the girls in our refuge, resulted in a ROI that no amount of money could ever buy.

Positive ROI in relationships means investing time, effort, and care into connections that yield mutual benefits. Strong relationships provide a network that becomes the basis for emotional support and creates a sense of belonging. This investment can lead to increased happiness, reduced stress, and improved mental health. Just like the long term relationship with my friend who wrote the check for that van, positive relationships stimulate personal and professional growth through collaboration, trust, and shared experiences, making the time and energy spent on them highly rewarding and impactful in the long run.

By investing in activities that align with your strengths and passions, you will achieve a greater sense of fulfillment and purpose. This alignment contributes to increased productivity and vigor in pursuing your goals. Learning to leverage these attributes tends to yield superior results, driving career advancement, financial rewards, and overall success.

Professionally, the ROI is enhanced performance, recognition, and opportunities. Personally, it is a sense of purpose, meaning, and fulfillment in life.

Finding your sweet spot transcends mere success or achievement. It encompasses a holistic alignment of passion, purpose, uniqueness, wisdom, abilities, and many other characteristics that secure your desired ROI in a variety of areas. This will also likely enhance longevity in your chosen field of endeavor and even your life.

Expanding Your Repertoire

Your sweet spot does not have to limit you to a tiny field of operation. You owe it to yourself to consider its versatility and capabilities. This is the very essence of growth and relevance. Standing firm in the familiar does not mean standing still – it is about using your expertise to flourish.

Explore the evolution of musical pioneers like the talented Tom Jones, who consistently produced captivating performances that redefined his artistry. Embracing change, he expanded his horizons, enhancing his craft as the years went by. Jones was able to put his own stamp on classics, ranging from the soaring melodies of *"The Green Green Grass of Home"*[22] to the immersive rhythms of *"Kiss"* by Prince[23] - forging a unique career that has impacted the music industry since the early 1960's.

Rather than mirroring another style, Jones chose to embrace the unknown, expanding his repertoire with precision and flair. It is not about imitation; it's about discovering your own unique path and mastering your craft in a world of limitless possibilities.

Many artists become well known for a unique style or expression of their craft. The same is true of entrepreneurs and businesspeople. Every now and then, someone comes along that has learned and demonstrated the value of staying in their sweet spot while expanding their repertoire. Think of people like Elton John, Leonardo DaVinci, Michaelangelo, and Elon Musk – to name a few.

Finding and working in your sweet spot is not about being a jack of all trades. But there is nothing stopping you from growing that sweet spot and becoming more effective than you ever realized was possible.

---

[22] ©1965 Curly Putman Publisher: Sony/ATV Music Publishing LLC, Universal Music Publishing Group

[23] © 1986 Prince Controversy Music, USA.Universal/MCA Music Limited.

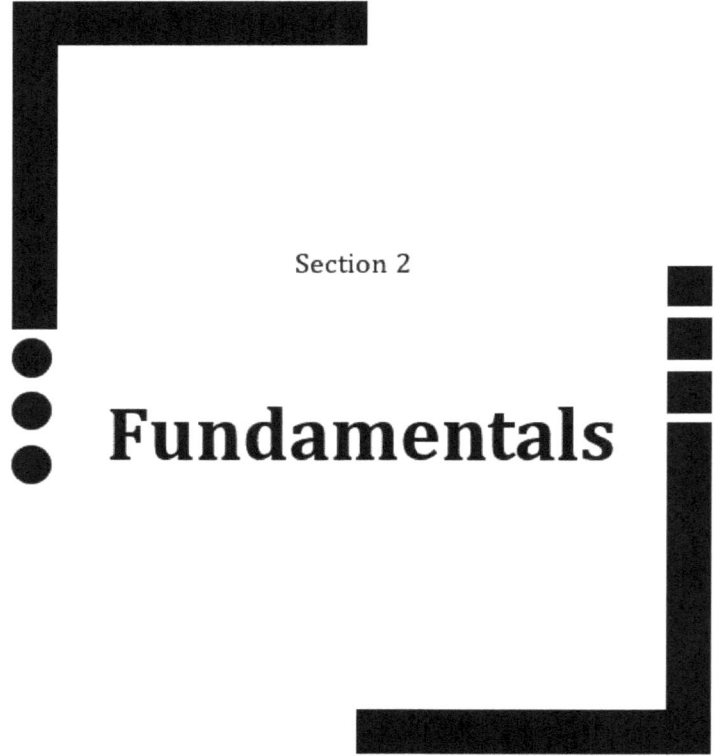

Section 2

Fundamentals

In the iconic film "The Karate Kid,"[24] the journey of Daniel LaRusso from a novice outsider to a skilled martial artist offers keen insights into the importance of life's fundamentals. Through the teachings of his mentor, Mr. Miyagi, Daniel learns that mastery is not merely about technique but also about character and discipline. As the narrative unfolds, we uncover the timeless wisdom embedded within the story, illustrating the transformative power of fundamentals in shaping our lives.

At the outset of "The Karate Kid," Daniel is depicted as a teenager grappling with the challenges of adolescence and acclimating to an unfamiliar environment. Bullied by his peers and struggling to find his place in a new town, Daniel's life is devoid of direction and purpose. It is only when he encounters Mr. Miyagi, a wise and enigmatic martial arts master, that Daniel's journey takes a transformative turn.

Under Mr. Miyagi's guidance, Daniel learns the importance of fundamentals. Through mundane tasks such as waxing cars, painting fences, and sanding floors, Daniel discovers that mastery is built upon the foundation of disciplined effort and focused dedication. Each repetition hones his skills till they become instinctive without him realizing it. Anyone familiar with the story and dialogue of the movie will remember the phrase, "Wax on, wax off," and how this became an intrinsic part of his proficiency in karate.

In a world characterized by instant gratification and fleeting success, Daniel's journey serves as a poignant reminder that true mastery is improved through patience and perseverance. Our dreams

---

[24] The Karate Kid. released by Columbia Pictures in 1984. Produced by Jerry Weintraub and directed by John G. Avildsen, it stars Ralph Macchio as Daniel LaRusso, Mr. Miyagi, played by Pat Morita. The success of the original film led to several sequels, a 2010 remake, and the popular series *Cobra Kai*, which continues the story in a modern setting, focusing on the rivalry between Daniel LaRusso and Johnny Lawrence, the main antagonist from the original film.

and aspirations require time to flourish and mature, unlocking the potential for sustained growth and enduring fulfillment.

"The Karate Kid" serves as a timeless parable of the transformative power of discipline and patience, in overcoming challenges and achieving mastery. As we embark on the journey of discovery of our sweet spots in our own lives, let us heed the wisdom of embracing the fundamentals that propel us towards our dreams and aspirations.

"The dictionary is the only place where "success" comes before "work"."

Mark Twain

Author

CHAPTER 7
The Journey to Overnight Success

Myths and Realities

In the age of instant gratification and overnight sensations, the expression, "It takes years of hard work to become an overnight success," bears repeating. Behind every seemingly sudden rise to fame or fortune lies a narrative of perseverance, dedication, and relentless pursuit of excellence. The myth of overnight success needs to be deconstructed, and the intricate interplay between effort, opportunity, and timing needs to be re-examined to define one's sweet spot in work and life.

The notion of overnight success is often romanticized in popular culture, portrayed as a stroke of luck or a sudden breakthrough that propels someone from obscurity to prominence in a flash. However, a closer examination reveals that such narratives rarely capture the full scope of the journey towards achievement. Behind the scenes, countless hours of toil, sacrifice, evaluation, and elimination lay the foundation for what appears to be a miraculous accomplishment.

Right Place, Right Time

One of the defining characteristics of overnight success stories is the element of timing. Opportunities seldom arise in isolation. Most often, they emerge at the convergence of preparation and opportunity. Those who achieve rapid success often find themselves in the right place at the right time, poised to capitalize on emerging trends, market dynamics, or cultural shifts. For the odd few, luck may play a role in opening doors, but it is worth working on the truism that the harder you work, the luckier you get. It is the preparedness and readiness to seize the moment that distinguishes true achievers from mere bystanders.

Much like in the case of Steve Jobs', the intersection of preparation and opportunity played a pivotal role. Let's take a closer look at his journey. In 1976, Jobs co-founded Apple in his parents' garage with Steve Wozniak, just as the personal computer revolution was beginning. Jobs' vision and marketing acumen, combined with Wozniak's technical expertise, led to the creation of the Apple I and, later, the Apple II, which became immensely successful. Their early entry into the burgeoning tech industry allowed Apple to become a leading company, revolutionizing personal computing and later, the smartphone industry with the iPhone. Apple would go on to become the first trillion-dollar company in history. Jobs' timing and strategic decisions were crucial to this success.

Facing Challenges

The concept of demanding work encompasses far more than sheer, dogged effort. It entails a commitment to growth, self-improvement, and a willingness to embrace the challenges inherent in the pursuit of excellence. Overnight success stories are often punctuated by moments of setback, failure, and adversity, each serving as a catalyst for learning and change.

Oprah Winfrey's journey to success is a powerful example of overcoming adversity. Born into poverty in rural Mississippi, Oprah faced numerous hardships, including abuse and neglect during her childhood. Despite these challenges, she excelled in school and won a scholarship to Tennessee State University. Her early career in media was fraught with difficulties, but her perseverance led her to a breakthrough as a talk show host in Chicago.[25]

---

[25] Kelley, Kitty (2010). Oprah: A Biography. Crown Publishing Group.

"The Oprah Winfrey Show" became a massive success, transforming her into a media mogul. Oprah's relentless work ethic, coupled with her ability to connect with and inspire audiences, paved the way for her to build a media empire that includes television networks, magazines, and philanthropic initiatives. She faced personal and professional obstacles, but her authenticity and dedication enabled her to become one of the most influential and successful women in the world.

The path to success is seldom linear but rather characterized by twists, turns, and unexpected detours. For myself, it has come through sometimes bitter experiences, sometimes unexpected delight and everything in between. On my personal journey I have had to navigate uncertainty, ambiguity, and self-doubt with unwavering resolve and clarity of purpose. In the face of obstacles, I found I had to draw upon my inner strength, determination, and passion to persevere against the odds.

Commitment to Success

The attainment of "overnight success" is often preceded by years of painstaking preparation and groundwork. Behind every breakthrough lies a wealth of experience, expertise, and mastery accumulated through much-dedicated practice, experimentation, and refinement. Whether in the realms of art, athletics, entrepreneurship, or academia, mastery requires a relentless commitment to honing your craft and pushing the boundaries of possibility.

Having a passionate interest in music, I have had the exciting privilege to go into a recording on a few occasions to work on projects for others and myself. Sure there are times when I walked in and recorded my part in one or two takes. The truth is that even the most experienced session musicians will work at recording a part many times so they can get it sounding just right. Often, the producer will make a composite final track made up of many phrases from different takes. This happens far more often the people realize and the result is a highly polished product that seldom, if ever, is reproduced in live performances. My point is that success takes time and effort.

Author JK Rowling of Harry Potter fame faced struggles as a single mother living on welfare who battled to make ends meet. During this time, she worked on her writing, while coping with depression and financial difficulties. Her manuscript for the first volume was rejected by twelve major publishers before a relatively small publishing house, Bloomsbury, accepted it.[26] Once published, the book gained unforeseen popularity, and was awarded many prestigious awards, which resulted in the series selling over 500 million copies worldwide.

Going Viral

The proliferation of social media has fueled the myth of overnight success, perpetuating the notion that fame and fortune can be achieved with a single viral post or moment of brilliance. While social media platforms offer unprecedented opportunities for visibility and exposure, they also amplify the pressure to perform and conform to idealized standards of success. The reality, however, is far more nuanced and multifaceted.

The cult of overnight success obscures the arduous journey that precedes it, glossing over the years of hard work, sacrifice, and perseverance that pave the way for momentous achievements. Behind every viral story or overnight sensation lies a tapestry of

---

[26] Smith, Sean (2001). JK Rowling: A Biography. Michael O'Mara Books

trials and tribulations, victories, and defeats, each contributing to the narrative of growth and preparation.

Charli D'Amelio[27] achieved viral status on social media through hard work and strategic use of platforms. Starting in mid-2019, Charli began posting dance videos on TikTok, quickly gaining traction due to her relatable content, consistent posting, and engaging personality. Her ability to participate in trending challenges and collaborate with other popular creators also contributed to her rapid rise in popularity.

Charli's dedication to producing high-quality content daily, interacting with her audience, and maintaining a genuine presence helped her amass millions of followers in a short period. Her viral success was not just a result of luck but also her persistent efforts to stay relevant and connected with her fans. She leveraged her social media fame to secure brand deals, launch her own merchandise, and even venture into traditional media, showcasing how hard work and strategic planning can lead to viral success.

Paying the price

Chasing overnight success often comes at a cost you don't realize until it's too late. It can take a toll on mental health and well-being, promoting unrealistic expectations, comparison, and something known as imposter syndrome.[28] The relentless quest for validation and external recognition can overshadow well-intentioned motivations and core values. Sometimes, it can lead you down a path

---

[27] https://www.businessinsider.com/charli-damelio-100-million-followers-tiktok-2020-11

[28] Imposter syndrome is a psychological pattern where individuals doubt their accomplishments and fear being exposed as frauds. Despite evident success, those experiencing it often feel undeserving and attribute their achievements to luck rather than skill or competence. It can affect self-esteem and professional performance.

of disillusionment and potentially lead to burnout. In the pursuit of greatness, it is essential to nurture a sense of balance and perspective, recognizing that success is not defined by momentary external accolades but by the journey itself.

Howard Schultz, who had three terms as CEO of Starbucks[29], paid a great price to achieve success. Growing up in a poor family in Brooklyn, Schultz worked various jobs to support his education. When he joined Starbucks in the 1980s, he envisioned transforming it from a small coffee bean retailer into a global café chain. To realize this vision, Schultz faced immense financial risk, even mortgaging his home to buy the company. He worked long hours, often at the expense of his personal life, to expand Starbucks. Schultz's determination and willingness to take significant personal and financial risks were crucial to his success.

Conclusion

In my line of work I have engaged with many individuals and groups. Some engagements have resulted in success beyond our expectations. Some, by any normal metrics, have been unmitigated disasters. I could shrug my shoulders and say, That's life," indeed I have done so on a few occasions. My point is that it's the successes and failures that make up the profound journey of growth, discovery, and self-realization and underpins true achievement. Behind every triumph lies a narrative of perseverance and unwavering commitment to excellence. By embracing the process and the journey, you can find meaning and fulfillment in the pursuit of your loftiest aspirations. As you navigate the complexities of life, remember that true success is not measured by the destination but by the depth of experience, growth, and transformation along the way.

---

[29] 1986 – 2000; 2008-2017; Interim CEO 2022-2-23.

Personal Challenge

To stay on track and achieve your purpose, here are three key points to keep in mind.

1. Milestones and Monuments

   Break down your ultimate purpose into smaller, actionable goals with specific deadlines. This not only makes your purpose more tangible but also provides a roadmap to follow, keeping you focused and motivated.

2. Assess and Adjust

   Periodically assess your progress and reflect on whether your actions align with your purpose. This allows you to make necessary adjustments, ensuring that you remain on course and adapt to any changes or challenges that arise.

3. Decide and Discipline

   Establish daily or weekly routines that support your goals. Consistency is crucial in building momentum, and disciplined habits will keep you moving forward, even when motivation wanes.

"A ship in harbor is safe, but that is not what ships are made for."

John A. Shedd

Author

.

CHAPTER 8
Beyond Comfort

Comfort is enticing. It is a warm, cozy bubble where everything feels familiar, safe, and predictable. We all seek comfort in various aspects of our lives, whether it is in relationships, careers, or daily routines. However, while the comfort zone provides a sense of security, it can hinder personal growth and stifle creativity. Moving out of perceived security is essential for growth and self-discovery. Finding and living in your sweet spot will often mean venturing beyond your familiar spaces. It is essential for meaningful progress and fulfillment.

The Illusion of Security

At its core, the comfort zone represents familiarity and stability. It is where routines are established, risks are minimized, and anxiety is kept at bay. However, this sense of security can easily become a double-edged sword. While it guards you against immediate discomfort, it also shields you from new experiences, challenges, and opportunities for growth. By clinging to this sense of safety, you inadvertently stunt your personal and professional growth, settling for mediocrity instead of embracing the unknown.

As mentioned previously, I have been involved in helping out with a refuge for trafficked women in India for about a decade now. The couple that began this project are very middle class, people who have never been involved in this side of life. I have known them since we were kids. In their fifties, they saw a need and felt a strong sense of responsibility that they should do something about it. They had to move completely outside of the things that were familiar to them and began to learn about how to help these young ladies - many of whom were abused and forcibly put in the "trade" as young as 11 or 12 years of age.

Over the years, my organization has raised money for them and helped spread the word about the need for places like this. We have lost count of the hours spent talking and weeping about each girls story. One was kidnapped and sexually assaulted over a period of three days by a gang of thugs; another was the victim of incest and had two children before she turned sixteen; one girl that came to us was born and raised in a brothel and was literally eaten by rats while her mother plied her trade across the room. The stories are endless and the problem seems like there is no end. But because of people like this who are willing to go to a place way beyond their comfort zone, the girls that have come through our refuge have been educated, trained and in gainful employment. A couple of them are even married with children of their own.

Venturing beyond your perceived safe space exposes you to new experiences and challenges and requires adaptability and courage. The security you feel in familiarity can be an illusion. True security does not come from maintaining the status quo but from your ability to navigate and thrive in the unknown. Embracing discomfort and uncertainty can lead to significant advancement, opening doors to opportunities that you might never encounter if you remain confined by your sense of ease. Real progress demands stepping out of our perceived safe-havens.The rewards can impact many and bring about a new perspective on your purpose.

Stagnation and Complacency

Growth requires discomfort and a level of grit in the face of uncertainty. By settling for what is comfortable, you rob yourself of the chance to explore your full potential and reach new heights of achievement.

Stagnation and complacency are significant threats to both personal and professional development, often leading to a decline in growth and potential. When individuals or organizations become complacent, they may fall into a state of passivity, satisfied with the status quo. This mindset discourages innovation, learning, and improvement, which are essential for long-term success and adaptability.

When considering your personal development, stagnation can lead to a lack of fulfillment and purpose. Without setting new goals or challenging yourself, life can become monotonous, reducing motivation and enthusiasm. This can result in missed opportunities for growth, as you may fail to acquire new skills, expand your knowledge, or explore different perspectives. Over time, this stagnation can lead to a decrease in self-esteem and a feeling of being stuck, further inhibiting progress.

Professionally, complacency can be particularly damaging in a rapidly changing world. Industries evolve, and new technologies and methodologies emerge. Those who do not continuously develop their skills and adapt to these changes risk becoming obsolete. This not only hampers career advancement but can also lead to job loss in more competitive environments. In addition, complacency within organizations can stifle creativity and innovation, leading to a decline in initiative and market relevance.

Ultimately, the dangers of stagnation and complacency lie in their ability to erode ambition and create a false sense of security. To thrive personally and professionally, it is crucial to embrace challenges and remain open to new opportunities for change and growth. Getting back to our girls from the refuge, even though some of them have graduated and have passed through the program, we are looking at another phase to take them to a whole new level of being productive members of society that will not only have a story to tell but will somehow be key players in preventing the evil of human sex trafficking from scarring the next generation. This is going to take another huge step beyond the current comfort zone.

By stretching yourself beyond a place of ease and complacency, you will continue to grow, sustain momentum and avoid the pitfalls of stagnation.

Fear of Failure

Fear often lurks at the edge of the comfort zone, whispering tales of potential failure and embarrassment. It's natural to be apprehensive about stepping into the unknown, but succumbing to this fear only perpetuates stagnation. Failure is an inevitable part of the learning process, and every setback presents an opportunity for growth and discovery. By embracing failure as a stepping stone rather than an obstacle, we build the courage to pursue our dreams outside the confines of our comfort zone. (We will examine the subjects of failure and fear in later chapters).

Limited Learning and Innovation

Within the comfort zone, learning and innovation find stagnation. Growth thrives on novelty and challenge, both of which are scarce commodities when you settle for where you are at. True learning occurs when we venture into uncharted territory, confront unfamiliar ideas, and adapt to new environments.

In July 2000, my wife and I moved from Australia to the USA. This meant crossing an entire ocean and moving half a world away. There were several factors that went into making that decision a positive one but the one thing that made us apprehensive was the unknown. Family, church, and familiarity with where we had grown up were all extremely important aspects of our lives. In addition, I was self-employed and the specter of not making enough money loomed as a very large, very real possibility.

Considering these factors made us hesitate despite all the positive things that this move presented. After much prayer and planning, we realized we could not only be selling ourselves short, but we could be hindering development opportunities for our then-teenage sons. It is fair to say that I would not have accomplished many of the things I have today if we had allowed any of those factors that prevent us from stepping beyond the limits of our comfort levels.

Innovation flourishes when you dare to question the status quo, challenge orthodoxy, and explore unusual solutions. By venturing beyond your comfort zone, you unlock new avenues for creativity and innovation that would otherwise remain unexplored.

Embracing Discomfort

Contrary to popular belief, discomfort is not synonymous with failure or misery. There is a dramatic difference between being anxious because of stress and stretching yourself because you are challenged. In fact, discomfort is often a sign of growth and progress. It is the feeling of going beyond your perceived limits, expanding your horizons, and embracing the full spectrum of your purpose in life. By reframing discomfort as a catalyst for growth rather than a deterrent, you empower yourself to transcend your limits and pursue your purpose with courage and determination.

While there are many similarities between life in Australia and life in the USA, we had to deal with the discomfort of dealing with the differences. Applying for a mortgage was a whole adventure of getting laughed out of banks when they discovered we did not have a credit score in the American system.

One of the most uncomfortable learning experiences came when our eldest son was diagnosed with Type 1 diabetes after only two weeks in the country. Australia has a nationalized public healthcare scheme, so the cost was a very minor consideration for the average family. Without medical insurance, the cost of hospitalization, testing kits, and insulin supplies increased very quickly. What we would normally manage with a phone call or a single visit to a government office now took many months of calling, interviews and a lot of apprehension as we navigated an insurance system that did not accept people with pre-existing conditions at that time. We even considered cutting our losses and heading back to Australia so we could live comfortably with the hand that had been dealt to us.

Thanks to the savvy of some very understanding social workers and hospital staff, we found a way to move forward. The outcome was worth the initial effort, and he is now an adult with a family of his own; his condition and cost of healthcare are managed, and he is living and working in his own sweet spot and achieving his dreams.

What could you accomplish if you dared to step out of your comfort zone?

Cultivating Resilience

Resilience is one of the foundation stones of personal and professional success. It is the ability to bounce back from difficult times, adapt to change, and thrive in the face of uncertainty. While the comfort zone offers temporary refuge from life's challenges, it also inhibits your ability to be resilient in the face of setbacks. By venturing beyond your comfort zone, you confront adversity head-on, learn determination, and fortify yourself to withstand life's inevitable storms.

Here are a few things I have done - and encouraged many others to do - to become more resilient.

1. Develop a Positive Mindset. Focus on what you can control and maintain a hopeful outlook by learning how to recognize and avoid negativity. This mindset builds mental toughness and helps you navigate adversity. Personally, I absolutely

despise negativity and move to shut it down the moment I recognize its presence. I have seen too many dreams go unfulfilled because of a negative attitude.

2. Build Strong Relationships. Surround yourself with supportive friends, family, and mentors. Strong relationships provide emotional support, perspective, and encouragement during tough times, enhancing your ability to bounce back from adversity and stay on purpose. There were many factors that helped make our move from Australia to the USA a successful exercise. The main factor was an strong base of relationships that helped us navigate the unknowns.

3. Practice Self-Care Prioritize physical health through regular exercise, balanced nutrition, and sufficient sleep. Engage in activities that help reduce stress, such as hobbies and spiritual pursuits. A healthy body, mind, and spirit are crucial for enduring and overcoming challenges. For many - especially myself - this is an ongoing challenge.

Beyond Boundaries

True fulfillment lies beyond the boundaries of your comfort zone. It is found in the thrilling journey of personal and professional discovery, the pursuit of meaningful goals, and the embrace of life's myriad experiences. Familiarity may offer fleeting moments of contentment, but it pales in comparison to the profound exhilaration that comes from pushing your limits. It is when you are able to go beyond these confines that you find yourself overcoming obstacles and realizing your purpose.

While the comfort zone may offer a temporary refuge from life's uncertainties, it is not your sweet spot. It's a comfortable prison that confines you to normality, stifles your growth, and limits your potential. To truly thrive and lead a fulfilling life, you must embrace discomfort, challenge yourself to venture beyond the familiar, and embrace the transformative power of discovery and growth. Only then can you break free from the shackles of mediocrity, discover your sweet spot, and unlock the boundless opportunities that await you in the vast expanse of the unknown?

Personal Challenge

To avoid stagnation and being stuck in your comfort zone in work and life:

1. Continually seek growth and challenge. Once you have achieved your goal, look for a fresh challenge.

2. Surround yourself with motivated, inspiring people who challenge and support you. We all need someone who will throw down the gauntlet from time to time so we can grow.

3. Reflect on your progress and adjust your strategies as needed. Going beyond your comfort zone means you have not done it before, which will require moderating old strategies.

The goal is to grow and not become stagnant or settled in your ways. Look for how you can be better.

"Failure is simply the opportunity to begin again, this time more intelligently."

Henry Ford

Founder, Ford Motor Company

CHAPTER 9
Failures on the Road to Success

A few years ago, a friend asked me if I had any regrets in life. After thinking about it for a few minutes, I realized that I had made my share of mistakes and had quite a few failures. Curiously, I had few regrets. I passionately believe it is because I was taught at an early age to own my mistakes, get the help I need, and move on.

Over the years, I have missed opportunities, made bad financial decisions that resulted in debt. Though we are debt free now, I realize our financial position would be vastly different if I had made better choices earlier in my life. One such experience was when we were given the option to purchase the apartment we were renting at the time for $54,000. We didn't have the $5000 deposit back then and in hindsight, I could have made a better effort to try and raise the money. I did not see my life plan as being compatible with the responsibility of home ownership. I have learned since then, that the purchase of that property would have been an investment instead of a hindrance to my dreams. In 2019 I walked by that place on a visit to Australia and we noticed the apartment was valued at well over $600,000.

I have also said and done things that I would have been better off not saying or doing, and a laundry list of other things that set me back temporarily. Many of them could well have provided me with cause to give up, but looking back, I realize they became the building blocks for my future.

Stumbling Blocks into Steppingstones

Failures are often perceived as obstacles or roadblocks that obstruct the path to success. However, when viewed from a higher perspective, failures reveal themselves to be integral checkpoints on the journey towards achievement. They serve as crucial milestones, guiding you through the intricate terrain of growth, learning, and discovery. Embracing failure as part of the process enables you to move beyond your limitations, adjust your outlook, and realize your fullest potential.

The notion that failures are checkpoints on the road to success lies in the recognition that failure is not an endpoint but rather a stepping stone toward progress. Each setback presents an opportunity for reflection, recalibration, and refinement. It prompts you to evaluate your strategies, reassess your goals, and refine your approach. In doing so, when you respond correctly to failure, you develop perseverance, and adaptability - qualities that are indispensable if you are to live with purpose.

While it's clear that failures can be steppingstones, it's also essential to face them head-on. This requires more than just recognizing their value—it involves confronting the fear and uncertainty that accompanies them."

Confronting Failure

It is important to remember that the journey from failure to success is not devoid of challenges and dilemmas. The fear of failure looms large, casting a shadow of doubt and hesitation over the aspirations of many. The stigma attached to failure, particularly in circles that valorize achievement and success, often leads people to conceal their setbacks and struggles, fearing ridicule and rejection. Yet, it is precisely in acknowledging and confronting these fears that you unlock the transformative potential of failure, moving beyond the limits of the moment and unleashing your undiscovered reservoirs of determination and creativity.

Confronting failure begins with accepting it as a natural part of the learning process. Instead of dwelling on the negative, analyze what went wrong to identify areas for improvement. Use this insight to develop new strategies and refine your approach for future challenges. View each setback as a step towards growth rather than a final defeat. Seek feedback from others to gain new perspectives and stay focused on your long-term goals. By treating failure as a valuable learning experience, you can turn it into an opportunity to build strength, adaptability, and success.

Calamity to Catalyst

Contrary to common misconceptions, failure does not always mean defeat; rather, it can become a trigger point for growth and innovation. History abounds with cases of those who encountered failure repeatedly before achieving remarkable success. Early in his career, Walt Disney was fired from a newspaper job for "lacking creativity" and faced bankruptcy after the failure of his first business venture. He later created Disney Studios and built one of the most successful entertainment empires in the world.[30]

Failure also serves as a potent catalyst for personal and professional maturity. It compels you to confront your limitations, move beyond your comfort zones, and venture into new territories. Embracing failure as a teacher rather than a tormentor helps you to see opportunities for growth instead of defeat. The right approach is to be open to feedback, willing to take risks, and commit to continuous improvement.

One of the often-overlooked aspects of failure is that it can come with emotional benefits by breeding humility and empathy. This, in turn, instills in you a profound appreciation for the struggles and

---

[30] Barrier, Michael (2007). The Animated Man: A Life of Walt Disney. University of California Press.

setbacks inherent in the pursuit of excellence. It builds a sense of understanding, as you recognize that failure is a universal experience, rising above boundaries of age, gender, and background. By acknowledging and sharing your failures in the right way, you help generate an environment of mutual support and encouragement, where setbacks are viewed not as sources of shame but as opportunities for collective growth and learning.

Explorer to Entrepreneur

In the realm of entrepreneurship and innovation, failure assumes a particularly pivotal role. The small business ecosystem is replete with tales of ventures that faltered and fizzled out, only to rise from the ashes stronger, wiser, and more robust. Silicon Valley, often heralded as the epicenter of technological innovation, echoes with stories of founders who weathered countless setbacks and rejections before achieving unprecedented success. In this dynamic environment, failure is not merely tolerated but celebrated as a rite of passage, a badge of honor that distinguishes those who dare to dream from those who shy away from risk.

When managed correctly, failure also helps encourage exploration and entrepreneurship. This becomes a place where creativity flourishes, and boundaries are pushed beyond conventional limits. It is where you are liberated from the shackles of perfectionism, encouraging you to embrace the opportunity to strive for excellence. In this fertile setting, seeds of innovation take root, growing into groundbreaking ideas, products, and solutions that transform industries and redefine the contours of personal and professional opportunity.

How Failure helps

1. Failure prompts a reassessment of our existing model or worldview. Thomas Edison had 10,000 failures in his effort to invent the lightbulb. When questioned about this, his response was, "I have not failed 10,000 times – I've successfully found 10,000 ways that will not work."

2. Failure helps us define our limitations and whether we can move beyond them. When we fail because we hit a limitation, we need to stop and reflect on whether that limit was self-imposed - and work to extend beyond it - or if we have reached the end of what we can do.

3. Failure helps us empathize with others. I've learned over the years that failure has deepened my empathy for others, allowing me to connect with their struggles in more meaningful ways."Understanding what others go through gives us a greater capacity to speak into their struggles and help them find a way through.

4. Failure can help us become more aware of our true destiny. Our successes and failures should guide us to a place where we are more aware than ever of our true purpose and guide us away from that which distracts us from it.

5. Failure can help form alliances with those who demonstrate strengths in our areas of weakness. Once we recognize we cannot do everything, it is important to "staff our weaknesses." This is not to make us dependent on others but rather interdependent.

6. Failure is an opportunity to reflect on what, how, and why we went wrong. When trying to make sense of any scenario, don't hesitate to use some or all of those "Six Honest Serving Men" (see Chapter 26) to help evaluate the situation.

7. Failure can motivate us to reprioritize our lives. Failure has the power to inspire us to reassess our priorities, redirecting our focus toward what truly motivates and fulfills us with renewed determination.

Conclusion

Pulling this together, failures are not obstacles to success but rather indispensable milestones on the road to living your purpose and defining your sweet spot. They serve as catalysts for growth, innovation, and discovery, propelling you toward your fullest potential. Learn to embrace failure as a natural and inevitable part of the journey. In the tapestry of human experience, failures need not be marks of shame but badges of courage, testifying to the indomitable spirit of those who dare to dream, dare to fail, and ultimately dare to succeed.

Personal Challenge

Dealing with failure effectively involves a three-step approach: reflect, recalibrate, and refine.

1. Reflect

    Begin by reflecting on the failure. Analyze what went wrong and why. Understanding the root cause helps you gain clarity and prevents you from repeating the same mistakes. Reflecting also allows you to acknowledge your emotions, which is important for moving forward constructively.

2. Recalibrate

    After understanding the reasons behind your failure, recalibrate your approach. This may involve adjusting your goals, changing your strategy, or improving your skills. Recalibration is about aligning your efforts with the lessons learned, ensuring that your next attempt is more informed and focused.

3. Refine

    Finally, refine your methods and mindset. Use the insights gained from reflection and recalibration to fine-tune your approach. Continuous refinement is key to personal and professional growth, transforming failure into a stepping stone towards success. It encourages adaptability and resilience, essential traits for long-term achievement.

"Multitasking is a lie. It's just task-switching and it makes you less efficient."

Gary Keller

Founder, Keller Williams Real Estate

CHAPTER 10
Reconsidering Multitasking

Modern culture is marked by perpetual busyness and relentless demands. The concept of multitasking has become almost synonymous with efficiency and productivity. From juggling multiple tasks at work to managing various commitments in personal life, the ability to multitask is often heralded as a valuable skill. However, beneath the surface lies a complex reality that challenges the glorification of this concept. We need to take a critical look at the phenomenon, exploring its implications, limitations, and potential alternatives.

Multitasking refers to the simultaneous handling of multiple jobs or activities at the same time. Proponents argue that multitasking enables individuals to accomplish more in less time, thereby enhancing productivity and efficiency. In today's fast-paced society, where time is a scarce resource, the allure of multitasking is undeniable. However, a closer examination reveals that all may not be as it seems.

In my own experience, and supported by research, I've seen how multitasking can create the illusion of productivity but often leads to burnout.

Cognitive Impairment

One of the primary concerns surrounding multitasking is its impact on cognitive functioning. Research in cognitive psychology has consistently demonstrated that the human brain is not designed to effectively manage multiple tasks[31] simultaneously. Instead, it

---

[31] Ophir, E., Nass, C., & Wagner, A. D. (2009). Cognitive control in media multitaskers. Proceedings of the National Academy of Sciences, 106(37)

operates more efficiently when focusing on one task at a time. When you attempt to multitask, cognitive resources become divided, leading to decreased performance and increased errors. This phenomenon, known as "task-switching cost," [32] highlights the inherent limitations of multitasking.

Managing many tasks at the same time can lead to negative effects on attention and concentration, and ultimately, the outcome. An article in Psychology Today magazine states that studies show a 40% reduction in productivity when people are trying to handle multiple tasks at the same time. They go on to say that even the term "multitasking" is a misnomer as the vast data available from research shown the brain can only focus on one task at a time. What we are actually doing when we think we are multitasking is more accurately "task switching." In fact, they found that something as simple as walking while talking on the phone increases the chance of bumping into someone or something. [33]

Modern culture is characterized by constant distractions and interruptions so maintaining focus has become increasingly challenging. The constant influx of emails, notifications, and other stimuli, fragments attention and impedes deep meaningful engagement with tasks at hand. As a result, multitaskers may find themselves trapped in a cycle of perpetual distraction, unable to devote their full cognitive resources to any single activity.

Mind Games

Beyond its cognitive implications, multitasking also has significant psychological and emotional consequences. The

---

[32] Rubinstein, J. S., Meyer, D. E., & Evans, J. E. (2001). Executive control of cognitive processes in task switching. Journal of Experimental Psychology: Human Perception and Performance, 27(4)

[33] Psychology Today. The True Cost of Multitasking. Susan Weinschenk Ph. D. Published September 18, 2012.

incessant need to juggle multiple responsibilities can contribute to feelings of being overwhelmed, stressed, and burned out. Rather than promoting a sense of accomplishment and fulfillment, scattered focus often nurtures a sense of dissatisfaction and inadequacy. The relentless pursuit of efficiency at the expense of well-being undermines the very essence of human flourishing.

I spend a great deal of my time working with leaders of nonprofit entities. Burnout rates in these types of organizations are notably high, often exacerbated by multitasking demands. Employees in these sectors frequently juggle multiple roles due to limited resources and high workloads.

I have noticed that the cause of burnout among clergy is rarely related to religious or doctrinal issues. It is usually because ministers are expected to handle many roles in their positions. When you add in factors like low income, being on call 24/7 - often in crisis conditions - on top of the "mundane" aspects of ministry there is a lot of task switching that goes on in the life of a member of the clergy.

In 2013, my two closest friends died within a month of each other - one from cancer and the other from a massive heart attack. I remember being in the Cardiac Unit of the hospital to offer what I could to the family, then stepping out to call the other family of the friend dying of cancer. All this was on top of having to prepare for the Sunday service and a host of other minor tasks that no one notices unless they are not done. There was not even time to process my own grief as my two closest friends in the world departed this life.

The pressure to meet diverse needs—such as fundraising, program management, and community outreach—without adequate support leads to chronic stress and fatigue. George Barna, of Barna

Research, published a survey that showed 38% of American clergy had seriously considered leaving the ministry because of the pressures in a post COVID world due to isolation, financial pressures resulting in often overwhelming workloads. This rate was higher for those under 45.[34] This environment raises the incidence of emotional exhaustion, diminished job satisfaction, and decreased productivity. Studies show that burnout rates in nonprofits can surpass those in for-profit sectors,[35] underscoring the need for improved work-life balance. Better resource allocation, and strategies to manage the work process go a long way to sustaining employee well-being and organizational effectiveness.

The result is the quality of work produced through multitasking is often compromised. While multitaskers may appear to be highly productive on the surface, the quality of their output may suffer due to divided attention and reduced cognitive processing. Tasks completed in a multitasking environment are more prone to errors, oversights, and omissions, diminishing their effectiveness and value.

Smarter Hard Work

In contrast to the prevailing narrative that multitasking is synonymous with productivity, recent research suggests that the opposite may be true.[36] Studies have shown that if you focus on one task at a time, you not only perform better but also experience greater satisfaction and fulfillment. By immersing yourself fully in

---

[34] https://www.barna.com/research/pastors-well-being/

[35] Goulet, L. R., & Frank, M. L. (2002). Organizational commitment across three sectors: Public, non-profit, and for-profit. Public Personnel Management, 31(2)

[36] Rubinstein, J. S., Meyer, D. E., & Evans, J. E. (2001). Executive control of cognitive processes in task switching. Journal of Experimental Psychology: Human Perception and Performance, 27(4)

the present moment, you cultivate a state of optimal experience characterized by deep concentration and focused motivation.

The saying "Work Smarter, Not Harder" originated in the 1930s from Allen F. Morgenstern,[37] an industrial engineer and the creator of the work simplification program. The program's intent was to increase the ability of people to produce more with less effort. Decades after its inception, the phrase has come to be seen by some as 'hard work is obsolete.' The concept suggests that efficiency and intelligence in your approach can replace the need for diligence and effort. While it contains some truth, it can be misleading if taken to extremes and used as a basis for multitasking.

One of the benefits that came out of the Covid crisis was the increase in the use of telemedicine. During the pandemic, doctors worked harder than they had before, but because they streamlined the processes they were able to achieve a lot more. Patient wait times and general function of the medical centers was streamlined. People in rural areas had easier access to medical care, and operational efficiency was generally increased across the medical industry.

True success often requires a combination of both smart and hard work. Efficiency strategies like using technology, and optimizing workflows are crucial. Yet, they can't entirely eliminate the need for sustained effort and dedication. Challenges often demand perseverance, and a willingness to put in the hours necessary to achieve mastery and meaningful results.

Oversimplification can lead to frustration when quick fixes do not yield desired outcomes. Ultimately, balancing smart strategies with a strong work ethic ensures comprehensive, sustainable success, debunking the myth that one can entirely replace the other.

---

[37] Morgenstern, A. F. (1932). Simplification of Work. New York: McGraw-Hill.

Now that we've examined the psychological impacts of multitasking, how can we work differently?

Micro-Tasking

Rather than striving to multitask, consider embracing the concept of micro-tasking — the practice of devoting your undivided attention to one task at a time, even if only for a brief period. Micro-tasking involves breaking down large projects into small, manageable tasks that can be completed quickly. This method is often more productive than multitasking because it allows for greater focus, efficiency, and quality of work.

1. Focused Attention. When you micro-task, you concentrate on a single task at a time. This focused attention reduces the cognitive load on your brain, enabling you to work more effectively. Multitasking, on the other hand, divides your attention across several tasks, leading to frequent switching between activities. As we have seen, this constant switching can create mental fatigue and decrease the quality of work by up to 40%.

2. Efficiency and Completion. Micro-tasking promotes efficiency by breaking down larger tasks into smaller, achievable steps. This makes it easier to track progress and maintain momentum, leading to quicker completion of each segment. Multitasking, however, often results in unfinished tasks, as attention is dispersed and progress on individual tasks may be slower.

3. Quality of Work. With micro-tasking, you can devote your full cognitive resources to each task, leading to a higher quality of work. Multitasking increases the likelihood of errors and overlooked details, as your brain struggles to juggle multiple activities simultaneously.

In essence, micro-tasking enhances productivity by fostering deep focus, ensuring efficient task completion, and maintaining high standards of work quality.

By prioritizing depth over breadth, you can develop the discipline to concentrate and be aware of the moment. Instead of succumbing to the tyranny of busyness, you can reclaim control over your time and energy, investing it in pursuits that truly matter to you.[38]

Conclusion

You must recognize the importance of setting boundaries and managing distractions in an increasingly connected world. By establishing designated periods of focused work and implementing strategies to minimize interruptions, we can create conducive environments for productivity and creativity to thrive. Embracing technologies that enhance rather than detract from our ability to concentrate can also play a pivotal role in our quest for single-mindedness.

The prevailing notion that multitasking is synonymous with efficiency and productivity warrants critical examination. While multitasking may offer the illusion of productivity, its inherent limitations and adverse effects on cognitive functioning, attention, and well-being cannot be ignored. By reevaluating your approach to work and embracing the principles of micro-tasking, you can sustain deeper engagement, greater satisfaction, and a more meaningful existence in an increasingly fragmented world.

As you navigate the complexities of modern life, remember that true productivity is not measured by the number of tasks you can juggle simultaneously, but by the excellence and the quality of your contributions to the world around you.

---

[38] For more help on micro tasking techniques, run a search on the internet for articles like this https//www.outsourceaccelerator.com/articles/microtasking/

Personal Challenge

Practice micro-tasking by making a list of all the things you need to get done in a day. Then, implement the following steps.

1. Start by identifying the main goals and then break them down into specific, actionable steps.

2. Use tools like to-do lists or task management software to organize these steps.

3. Set brief time limits for each task to maintain focus and productivity. Regularly review progress and adjust as needed to stay on track.

Track your results and compare them to previous productivity.

Edited to this point 10pm Sat Oct 5th.

"Personal relationships are the fertile soil from which all advancement, all success, all achievement in real life grows."

Ben Stein

American Writer, Lawyer

CHAPTER 11
Cultivate Relationships

I have never been enamored by celebrities. I prefer my relationships to be genuine with people that I can depend on when push turns to shove. In my work, I have met some famous people, but the ones who have stood by me in times of crisis are the ordinary everyday people with whom I have a genuine friendship.

In keeping with my love for music, at one point, I dabbled in concert promotions with an individual who was established in the industry. I was particularly looking forward to meeting one artist who was well-known in his field and had a great voice. Everything was set up according to his rider, and I was there to greet him when he arrived for the sound check. The guy turned out to be a jerk. He did his sound check, played his set, sold his product, and disappeared. Turns out that he was the same way with other promoters, his fame was short-lived, and even his marriage failed. I wasn't looking for a relationship with him, but it was soon apparent that he did not have many friendships of his own.

Cultivated relationships form the bedrock of personal and professional growth, offering sustenance, guidance, and support along the journey of life. It is important to understand the delicate balance of these connections. It shows a dynamic interplay of mentors, peers, and disciples, each contributing in unique ways to your development and well-being. Nurturing these relationships in the right proportions forms a rich montage of connections, promoting strength, wisdom, and fulfillment. Yet, tipping the scales too far in favor of one at the expense of others, risks undermining the very foundation upon which these relationships thrive.

John Donne was a 17th-century poet and cleric.[39] His poem "No Man is an Island" underscores the interconnectedness of people. It conveys that individuals are not self-sufficient and are designed to thrive within a community. Each person's actions and experiences impact others, reflecting our interdependence. This idea emphasizes the importance of relationships, empathy, and mutual support. By acknowledging our reliance on one another, we help promote cooperation, compassion, and cohesion. Donne's words remind us that isolation is detrimental, and that our well-being is achieved through unity and connection, illustrating the profound bonds that tie human beings together.

Three Levels of Relationships

In all facets of your life, you will find benefits in three main levels of relationship: Preceptors, Peers, and Protégés. While there may be times when there will need to be a greater emphasis on one than the others, they are all necessary for a balanced life.

PRECEPTORS are qualified and trusted advisors or teachers. With their wealth of experience, wisdom, and insight, they occupy a pivotal role in your journey of self-discovery and growth. They serve as beacons of guidance and correction, illuminating the paths that lead to success, fulfillment, and purpose. Through their mentorship, you glean invaluable lessons learned in the crucible of their own triumphs and tribulations. Their experience offers you a compass to help navigate the complexities of life with grace and wisdom. While some mentors will fulfill a momentary role, the true value of preceptors is in having them watch over your journey through to the intended goal.

---

[39] Donne, John. Devotions upon Emergent Occasions, and several steps in my Sickness. London: A. Mathewes for Thomas Jones, 1624. This work is in the public domain.

PEERS, on the other hand, form the scaffolding of support and camaraderie that sustains you through life's ebbs and flows. They are friends or coworkers that share social or professional status with you. Bound by shared aspirations, values, and experiences, they serve as confidants, collaborators, and companions on the journey of life. In the framework of peer relationships, you find a safe harbor amidst the storms of uncertainty, inspiration amid the depths of despair, and laughter amid the trials of adversity.

In the last chapter, I told the story of the unexpected death of my closest friend due to a massive heart attack. We had been friends for over 15 years and were there for each other as we faced some very dark times over the years. We were not just peers professionally, we had a lot in common and spent a lot of time socializing - even taking the odd vacation together. He always made people laugh and seemed to have a knack for putting people at ease. When we went out to eat, we would have a lot of fun making the wait staff wonder if we were funny or just plain nuts. Sometimes our wives had to step in to let them know we didn't really want them to go across the road and pick up a Big Mac while looking at their fancy Italian menu.

When it came time to address serious issues we were always able to work together because we knew we had each others backs. We talked everyday on the phone. No matter how serious an issue we had to address for our work, somehow we always ended up laughing about something. We loved to meet over lunch as he would find these hole-in-the-wall places that ended up serving delicious food. In private, I nicknamed him Sir Lunch-a-lot. It was a rare friendship that I have never quite been able to replace and it played a significant role in bringing me to where I am today.

While peers provide camaraderie, mentoring the next generation has offered me profound growth and insight.

PROTÉGÉS are those who are being advised or trained by you. Their fresh perspectives, boundless enthusiasm, and insatiable curiosity infuse your life with vitality, energy, and purpose – not to mention the occasional headache. They challenge your assumptions, expand your horizons, and invigorate your spirit with the spark of possibility. Through their discipleship, you rediscover the joy of learning, the wonder of exploration, and the magic of innovation, renewing your commitment to growth, transformation, and discovery.

I should take the time to mention that the results of working with protégés are not always immediately apparent. There have been a few that have flat-out rejected the things I tried to teach them. Over the years I have discovered the most important quality for a protégé is teachability. People that have a different opinion are not a problem; people who think their opinion is the only correct one are. In the early days of training people I would be crushed when people rejected my mentorship. Now I have learned to take the "win" when it comes my way and let the other stuff slide.

Each of these three groups require some level or depth of relationship. Get to know the person with whom you are dealing. People who come along with flashes of inspiration are wonderful and indeed necessary in life. But people who will only stay around in the good times do not help you build or grow anything. In finding your sweet spot, don't forget to help others discover theirs along the way.

Striking a Balance

While each of these relationships offers unique benefits and opportunities, an over-reliance on one at the expense of the others runs the risk of diminishing your effectiveness and limiting your potential. Too much focus on preceptors, for instance, may breed dependence and stifle innovation, as you become overly reliant on the guidance and approval of others. Conversely, an exclusive emphasis on peer relationships may lead to insularity and conformity, as you gravitate towards the safety of the familiar at the expense of the unknown. Likewise, an overabundance of protégés may promote a sense of entitlement and complacency, as you bask in the adulation of others without acknowledging the responsibilities that accompany leadership and influence.

The most striking thing I have found about relationships is that the right balance among preceptors, peers, and protégés requires a nuanced understanding of their respective roles and contributions. It takes a willingness to promote relationships that honor the dignity, autonomy, and agency of all parties involved. I can say with great certainty that it is imperative to foster a nurturing ecosystem of mutual respect and trust, where each member is valued for their unique perspectives, and contributions to the benefit of the whole.

Cultivate, Nurture, Foster

In cultivating relationships with preceptors, you must approach them with a degree of humility, receptivity, and an attitude of inquiry, recognizing that true mentorship is not about seeking answers but asking the right questions. Learn to be willing to embrace discomfort and challenge as you confront the shadows of your own limitations and strive towards the goal of your highest potential. By honoring the wisdom and experience of your mentors while remaining true to your own intuition and values, you build a partnership grounded in authenticity, integrity, and mutual respect.

Similarly, in nurturing relationships with peers, you must cultivate a spirit of collaboration, empathy, and opportunity, recognizing that true fellowship is not about competition but cooperation. It means celebrating the successes of others, supporting them through their struggles, and championing their aspirations with generosity and goodwill. By fostering an environment of trust, transparency, and mutual support, you create a sanctuary where all voices are heard, all perspectives are valued, and all contributions are honored.

Finally, in fostering relationships with protégés, always seek to embody the qualities of humility, and accountability, recognizing that true leadership is not about exerting power but empowering others. It entails leading by example, modeling the values and behaviors you wish to instill in others, and cultivating an ethos of excellence, innovation, and continual improvement. By nurturing the talents, passions, and aspirations of those you mentor, you sow the seeds of a brighter future, where everyone is empowered to realize their fullest potential and discover their sweet spot.

Conclusion

Cultivated relationships - grounded in the dynamic interplay of preceptors, peers, and protégés - form the cornerstone of personal and professional growth, offering sustenance, guidance, and support along the journey of discovering your sweet spot. By striking the right balance among these relationships, you nurture a rich network of connections that nourish the mind, body, and spirit. Through humility, empathy, and integrity, you honor the inherent dignity and worth of all people, recognizing that true fulfillment lies not in the pursuit of individual success but in bringing others on the journey with you.

See Appendix 5 for some thoughts on relationship dynamics.

Personal Challenge

Building strong relationships with preceptors, peers, and protégés involves different strategies tailored to each group. Here is a guide to help you develop these relationships:

1. **With Preceptors**

   - Seek Common Ground: Find mentors whose experiences and values align with your goals.

   - Be Proactive: Take the initiative to reach out and maintain regular communication.

   - Show Appreciation: Express gratitude for their time and insights.

   - Be Coachable: Be open to feedback and willing to act on their advice.

   - Offer Value: Find ways to offer value in return, helping with tasks, sharing resources, etc.

2. **With Peers**

   - Collaborate: Work together on projects or common interests.

   - Be Supportive: Offer help when they face challenges. Celebrate their successes.

   - Communicate Openly: Be transparent and honest in your interactions.

   - Network Together: Attend events, workshops, or seminars as a group.

   - Respect Boundaries: Understand and respect personal and professional boundaries.

3. With Protégés

- Be Accessible: Make yourself available for guidance and support.

- Lead by Example: Your actions will speak louder than your words.

- Tailor Your Guidance: Understand their individual needs and tailor your advice accordingly.

- Encourage Independence: Encourage them to think critically and make decisions on their own.

- Celebrate Progress: Celebrating progress keeps them motivated and engaged.

- Provide Constructive Feedback: Offer feedback that is specific, actionable, and delivered in a way that fosters growth rather than discouragement.

Developing these relationships takes time, patience, and consistent effort. However, the mutual growth and support you will gain from these connections can be incredibly rewarding.

Section 3

Inverse Proportionality

In mathematics and physics, there are certain variable quantities that are directly related to each other. We refer to these quantities as proportional. There are also certain variable quantities that are *inversely proportional* to each other. When one goes up, the other goes down, and vice versa. Mathematically, when it comes to inverse proportionality, the product of the two variables is usually constant.

For example, let us suppose you want to travel one mile. You could walk and take about twenty minutes. An Olympic-class runner could run that same distance in around four to five minutes. If you drove a car, you could cover the distance in one minute. The constant would be the 1 mile traveled. The variables would be the velocity you travel at, and the time it takes to cover the distance.

In principle, this concept can apply to our personal, professional, and social life. Finding your sweet spot in life will help you to achieve the things you want to or need to. You must figure out which variables are going to enhance the journey and those which will make it more difficult.

The constant we are aiming for could be:

- Professionally - work product, income level…
- Personally - family life, vacation, house…
- Financially - retirement fund, investment, education fund…

It is important to figure out what will enhance or diminish these constraints.

In finding and functioning in your sweet spot, it is important to understand the distinction between direct and inverse proportionality and its relationship to all the variables. While strength training may be good for your health, it has little to no bearing on your job performance as a statistical analyst. If you are an athlete, it has a direct relationship.

In this section, we will highlight a few variables in life that are inversely proportional to each other, and how to recognize and manage them. Of course, there are many more than mentioned here. The intent is to trigger your ability to recognize and process the issues.

"Every decision is a risk; every risk is a decision."

Guy Kawasaki

Silicon Valley Venture Capitalist

CHAPTER 12
The Duality of Decision-making

Many years ago, I would take teams of people overseas with me to help with charitable work in developing nations. This has involved medical teams to provide treatment in remote villages, building teams to help with reconstruction in Haiti after the 2010 earthquake, painting bathrooms in an orphanage in Guatemala, and many other projects.

A businessman acquaintance became interested in the work I was doing and expressed a desire to come with me on a future trip. Over lunch, he explained to me how he had made $19 million the previous year. As I laid out the opportunities I had planned for the coming year, I asked him which one he would be most interested in. I soon discovered that he had difficulty making decisions because he hedged in every way possible to avoid making a commitment. His final excuse was he needed to wait till his finances were in order so he could make a trip with me. None of the trips would have cost more than $2500. In all the years I have known him, he never did come with me.

Wishful Thinking and Rational Logic

In the nuanced process of decision-making, the interplay between wishful thinking and rational logic unveils a dynamic that influences outcomes, actions, and personal growth. Wishful thinking, characterized by doublemindedness and second-guessing, stands in stark contrast to rational logic, which is based on informed choices and accountability for their consequences. The inverse proportionality between wishful thinking and rational logic highlights how decision-making impacts the ability to live a purposeful life.

111

At the heart of wishful thinking lies a lack of clarity and conviction regarding one's goals, values, and priorities. People plagued by indecision may find themselves torn between external expectations and internal conflicts. The fear of failure, rejection, or disappointment looms large, casting a shadow of doubt and uncertainty over every choice and action.

The inability to decide manifests as a state of ambivalence, wherein a person grapples with competing desires, fears, and uncertainties. The fear of making the wrong choice, coupled with the possibility of its consequences, paralyzes them and impedes their ability to take decisive action. This wavering between conflicting options will most often manifest as hesitancy, procrastination, and sometimes paralysis, relegating them to a state of near-perpetual indecision. That said, it is true that some people's sweet spot is in having others direct them in what to do,

In contrast, rational logic serves as a guiding principle in decision-making, advocating for a systematic approach to problem-solving grounded in evidence, reason, and critical thinking. Rational decision-makers assess available information, weigh potential outcomes, and evaluate risks and rewards before arriving at a well-informed conclusion. By adhering to principles of logic and probability, the process serves to minimize bias, error, and irrationality in their decision-making.

Go Beyond Heuristics

The inability to make decisions is often fueled by cognitive biases and heuristics that distort perception and cloud judgment. Heuristics are mental shortcuts or rules of thumb that simplify decision-making and problem-solving by providing quick, approximate solutions, often based on past experiences or common patterns. While they can be efficient and useful, they may sometimes lead to biases or errors.

A heuristic or heuristic technique (*problem-solving*, *mental shortcut*, *rule of thumb*) is any approach to problem-solving that employs a pragmatic method that is not fully optimized, perfected, or rationalized, but is nevertheless "good enough".[40]

Cognitive bias is similar and tends to steer individuals to seek out information that confirms preexisting beliefs, reinforcing entrenched patterns of thinking and decision-making. These biases skew perceptions by overemphasizing recent or vivid experiences, leading to distorted risk assessments and less-than-optimal choices.

A person who has had one particularly unpleasant experience with an airline may decide to avoid using said airline again, even though they may provide a better route, price and timing to their destination. Defaulting to their bad experience often causes them to ignore many other factors that could help them make an informed decision and provide a much better option.

In contrast, rational logic encourages a person to transcend ingrained biases and embrace a more considered and systematic approach to decision-making. By leveraging a variety of analytical tools, rational decision-makers strive to moderate the influence of bias and emotion, relying instead on empirical evidence and logical reasoning to inform their choices. Through disciplined inquiry and critical assessment, they work to uncover hidden assumptions and anticipate potential consequences with greater clarity and precision.

In March of 2020, I was scheduled to speak at two leadership conferences and a number of other training sessions over a two week

---

[40] Rudolph Groner, Marina Groner and Walter F Bishop (1983). Handbook of Psychophysiology: Central and Autonomic Nervous System Approaches. Lawerence Erlbaum and Associates Publishers.

period in Zambia. I was five hours away from getting on the flight when then President Trump and Vice President Pence came on the TV to announce a lockdown due to COVID. Two years of planning and preparation dissolved as they announced that all but essential services would be suspended. Immediately, I was on the phone to my contact in Zambia and he informed me that the local leaders still wanted me to come as Zambia was still open.

After discussing the trip with my wife and the airline, I processed all the information at hand and decided to cancel the trip. The Zambian conference organizers were quite upset but I stood my ground based on the information I had - even though I really wanted to go. The next day, I heard from them. Zambia had gone into lockdown and flights into and out of that whole South African region were suspended. If I had given in to the emotion of the situation and left the previous day, I would have been caught in limbo somewhere in Africa and likely unable to get back home for a few months.

The inability to make decisions not only weakens confidence and autonomy, but can also breed a sense of helplessness and lack of progress. As opportunities pass by, and circumstances moderate, the indecisive person remains stuck in a state of relative paralysis, unable to seize the moment or chart a course of action. The pursuit of excellence and purpose becomes elusive, overshadowed by the specter of indecision and regret.

Of the few regrets I have in my life, they all seem to be caused by bad or irrational decisions. What is your experience?

Eroded Trust or Responsibility

Indecision erodes trust and credibility, both in oneself and in the eyes of others. Indecisive leaders breed uncertainty and distrust among their followers, undermining morale and organizational effectiveness. In personal relationships, indecision can strain trust and communication, creating a sense of insecurity that damages intimacy and connection.

Conversely, rational logic empowers you to assume ownership and responsibility for your decisions, regardless of the outcomes. Rather than submitting to the whims of fate or external circumstances, rational decision-makers recognize the agency they wield in shaping their destiny. They acknowledge that every decision carries inherent risks and uncertainties, yet they embrace the challenge with courage, conviction, and integrity.

Rational decision-making advances a culture of accountability and constant improvement, in which failures and setbacks are viewed as opportunities for learning and growth. Rather than assigning blame or deflecting responsibility, rational individuals reflect on their choices, identify areas for improvement, and adapt their strategies accordingly. They recognize that success is not defined by the absence of failure but by the adaptability and resolve displayed in the face of adversity.

The Cuban Missile Crisis of 1962 stands as a prime example of rational decision-making amid dire circumstances. Faced with the discovery of Soviet nuclear missiles in Cuba, President John F. Kennedy chose a naval blockade over immediate military action. Despite intense pressure for a more aggressive response, Kennedy and his advisors pursued a diplomatic strategy, weighing the catastrophic risks of nuclear war. Through careful negotiation, they reached an agreement with Soviet Premier Nikita Khrushchev, leading to the removal of the missiles and averting a potential nuclear conflict. This measured approach showcased rationality and prudence under extreme tension.[41]

Conclusion

The inverse proportionality between wishful thinking and rational logic illuminates the contrast between indecision and informed choice in the realm of decision-making. While indecision leads to doubt, uncertainty, and stagnation, rational logic promotes clarity, deliberation, and accountability. By transcending cognitive biases, embracing practical evidence, and assuming responsibility for your decisions, you can navigate the difficulties of uncertainty with confidence, flexibility, and integrity. As you confront the challenges and opportunities that life presents, you embark on a journey of growth and transformation guided by the principles of rationality and reason.

---

[41] Garthoff, Raymond L. (1989). Reflections on the Cuban Missile Crisis. The Brookings Insitiute.

Personal Challenge

How to make rational decisions:

1. **Gather and Evaluate Information**

   Start by collecting all relevant data and perspectives. Analyze the information considering both short-term and long-term consequences. Ensure that your sources are reliable and that you understand the potential risks and benefits of each option.

2. **Remove Emotional Bias**

   Recognize and separate your emotions from the decision-making process. While emotions can provide insight, relying solely on them can lead to impulsive decisions. Take a step back to assess the situation objectively, focusing on logic and reason.

3. **Weigh Options and Outcomes**

   List all possible options and their potential outcomes. Use tools like pros and cons lists to compare them systematically. Consider the impact of each choice on your goals, values, and people around you, aiming to choose the option that aligns best with the sweet spot of your purpose.

"Fear is a reaction; courage is a decision."

Winston Churchill

British Prime Minister

CHAPTER 13
Fear and a Sound Mind

The inverse relationship between fear and a sound mind[42] is Biblical in its origin, outworking, and importance. Regardless of your spiritual or religious convictions, there is a huge lesson to be learned by looking at how the prevalence of fear diminishes as the clarity of your mental faculties increases. While fear, in some cases, is a natural and instinctual response to perceived threats or dangers, allowing it to dictate your actions and outcomes can impede rationale and undermine your potential. A sound mind, grounded in reason, wisdom, and discernment, serves as a bulwark against the tyranny of fear, empowering you to navigate life's challenges with courage, determination, and clarity of purpose.

Most of us have seen this interaction play out on television or in movies. A firefighter enters a burning building, fear gripping his[43] heart. Despite the danger, his training kicks in, allowing his sound mind to take over. He assesses the situation, plans his movements, and navigates through the smoke to rescue trapped victims. His fear sharpens his focus, heightening his awareness of every detail.

This interplay between fear and a sound mind enables him to act decisively and safely, demonstrating courage and expertise. Fear keeps him cautious, while his sound mind ensures he follows protocol, highlighting the balance needed in this situation. Too much of one or the other can limit his ability to do his job, or worse, put him in danger.

---

[42] It is not this authors purpose to address the issue of mental illness or health. The concept of a sound mind as used here is a disciplined approach to processing the issues of our lives.
[43] Yes, I know women can be firefighters too.

A Proper Response to Fear

Have you ever felt the weight of fear pressing down on you, making even the simplest decisions seem insurmountable? Fear, in its many manifestations, influences our thoughts, emotions, and behaviors, often masquerading as self-preservation or prudence. Yet, beneath its veneer of rationality lies a potent force that can cloud your judgment with doubt, and obscure the path to fulfilling your purpose. Whether it manifests as fear of failure, fear of rejection, or fear of the unknown, its insidious grip can derail your ambitions, imprisoning you within the confines of what is perceived as safe zones and preventing you from finding your sweet spot.

It is important to note that the presence of fear does not exclude the possibility of a sound mind. Rather, it is your response to fear - the degree to which you allow it to govern your thoughts, emotions, and actions—that determines the quality of your processes and the trajectory of your life. A sound mind enables you to confront your fears with courage and composure, transforming them from harbingers of failure into opportunities for growth and achievement.

Consider standing atop a high building. The fear of heights may instinctively trigger a cascade of physiological and psychological responses, compelling you to retreat from the precipice and seek safety on solid ground. On the other hand, a sound mind recognizes the inherent dangers of being on the edge of a high building - not out of fear, but out of prudence, wisdom, and self-preservation.

Dealing With Adversity

Indeed, the inverse proportionality between fear and a sound mind is most evident in moments of adversity and hesitation, where the clarity of your mental faculties is put to the test. In the face of daunting challenges, a sound mind remains steadfast and resolute, undeterred by the specter of fear and firm in its commitment to

121

purpose and principle. It does not deny the existence of fear but rather moves outside of its limitations, drawing strength from within to confront adversity with grace and courage.

A sound mind also breeds a mentality of abundance and opportunity, reframing fear as a catalyst for growth and transformation. Rather than succumbing to the paralysis of fear, it harnesses its energy to fuel the fires of creativity and innovation. It views setbacks not as sources of shame or defeat but as opportunities for adaptation and renewal, embracing the challenge as an integral part of the journey towards success.

Helen Keller, born in 1880, lost her sight and hearing at 19 months due to an illness. Despite these adversities, she overcame her fears with the help of her devoted teacher, Anne Sullivan. Sullivan used innovative techniques to teach Keller language, starting with finger spelling words in her hand. This breakthrough enabled Keller to communicate and eventually learn to read and write using Braille.

Keller became the first deaf-blind person to earn a Bachelor of Arts degree, graduating from Radcliffe College in 1904. She devoted her life to advocacy, becoming a renowned author, speaker, and political activist. She championed causes such as disability rights, women's suffrage, and labor rights, leaving a profound impact on society and inspiring millions worldwide.[44]

Developing a Sound Mind

The development of a sound mind is not without its challenges and obstacles. The cacophony of external pressures and internal

---

[44] The World I Live In. C 2013 Duke Classics. First published in 1904. A collection of essays by Helen Keller

doubts often conspire to erode confidence, cloud judgment, and sow the seeds of doubt and insecurity. The relentless barrage of negative self-talk and perfectionism can obscure the light of reason, leaving us adrift in a dark sea of uncertainty.

This is not just theory for me. I have had to train myself to exercise rationality over many different experiences in my journey of life. Eventually, rational response has become like muscle memory and I find over and over again, defaulting to logic - even when I recognize fear starting to creep in.

In a later chapter, I discuss the use of asking the right questions to process your thoughts. You would do well to go through that section carefully and learn to apply the skill of questioning to develop a system that guides you into a rational response, rather than giving in to the irrationality of fear.

Developing rational thinking over fear-driven responses leads to more informed and balanced decisions. This approach reduces anxiety, as it emphasizes logic and reason over irrational fears. It also inculcates problem-solving skills, enabling people to address challenges more effectively. Ultimately, rational thinking will empower you to navigate complex situations with clarity and composure, improving overall mental and emotional well-being.

Conclusion

The inverse proportionality between fear and a sound mind underscores the transformative power of clarity, wisdom, and discernment in navigating life's tests and opportunities. While fear may be an often-encountered specter on the journey of life, it need not dictate your thoughts, emotions, and actions. Through the development of a sound mind grounded in reason, strength, and purpose, you can transcend the limitations of fear, embracing life's uncertainties with courage, grace, and authenticity on the journey to discovering your sweet spot.

Personal Challenge

In the face of life's challenges, the cultivation of a sound mind requires conscious effort, discipline, and self-awareness.

1. Establish disciplines and self-analysis that enhance clarity, focus, and emotional equilibrium. Plot a beginning point (where you are) and endpoint (where you want to be ideally), and then plot the steps you need to take to get from one to the other.

2. Build a growth attitude characterized by openness to feedback and willingness to embrace discomfort. This is going to involve exercising a lot of trust in the process and the people around you in your journey.

3. Surround yourself with mentors, peers, and allies who inspire, challenge, and uplift you. These are people who will not simply make you feel good; they should be available to help you process your concerns about your situation.

Doing this will help keep your thought process on track and deter you from allowing your mind to go to negative places.

"Keep moving ahead, because action creates momentum, which in turn creates unanticipated opportunities."

Nick Vujicic

Motivational Speaker

Life without Limbs

CHAPTER 14
The Dynamics of Effort and Momentum

The highs and lows of the human journey are a classic illustration of the relationship between effort and momentum. It serves as a guiding principle, driving both progress and transformation as you pursue your purpose. While conventional wisdom suggests that greater effort yields greater momentum, that is only partially true. As momentum builds, the amount of effort required to maintain that momentum diminishes. This paradoxical relationship challenges conventional notions of productivity and efficiency. A deeper exploration into the dynamics of this phenomenon brings a surprising clarity on how finding and working in your sweet spot makes life easier. To unravel this interplay, let us dissect the components of the momentum so you can apply the principles to your work and life in a practical way.

The Components of Momentum

Now bear with me for a moment, as I take you through a simple lesson in physics to help you better understand the principles of momentum.

Momentum, the driving force behind progress and change, is a multifaceted concept that encompasses both physical and metaphorical dimensions. It is the product of mass and velocity.

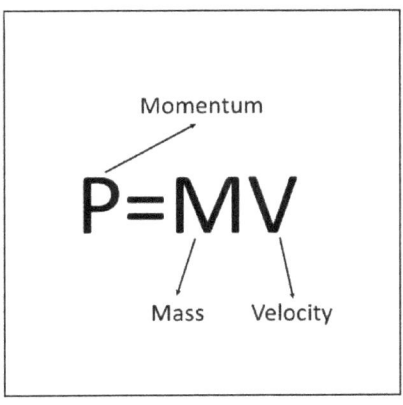

When velocity is applied to a mass or object, said object gains momentum. To achieve greater momentum, you could do a couple of things – increase the velocity or increase the mass of the object.

Velocity is different from speed. Speed denotes the rate of motion, measuring the distance covered per unit of time. Velocity adds a directional component, specifying both speed and direction, thus guiding the momentum in a specific direction toward desired outcomes. Time serves as the temporal backdrop against which momentum exists, defining its trajectory over intervals and shaping its sustainability.

In other words, the nature of momentum makes a variety of outcomes possible.

1. Right direction with low momentum

2. Wrong direction with high momentum

3. Right direction with high momentum

or a variety of other combinations – you get the idea.

Diminishing Effort

When applied to living your purpose, momentum transcends mere physical motion, permeating areas such as politics, business, education, and personal progress. Effort, the fuel that initiates momentum, plays a pivotal role in overcoming the resistance to commencing motion. However, the relationship between effort and momentum is not linear; rather, the more velocity you achieve, the more momentum you gain, and less effort is required to maintain that level of momentum. Initially, large efforts yield significant gains, building momentum and progressing in the desired direction.

With increasing momentum, the need for additional effort diminishes. Assuming there is little or no variable resistance, momentum becomes self-sustaining, continuing forward with reduced input. This inverse relationship between effort and momentum challenges traditional notions of productivity, suggesting that excessive effort may hinder rather than enhance progress. Instead of brute force, strategic leverage of momentum becomes vital, allowing individuals and organizations to achieve more with less effort – smarter hard work, as mentioned in Chapter 10.

The phenomenon of diminishing effort highlights the importance of strategic allocation of resources, careful prioritization of tasks, and adaptive approaches to problem-solving. Understanding these dynamics helps you to recognize when to capitalize on momentum and when to recalibrate. Strategies are essential for optimizing efforts and maximizing outcomes. By understanding the dynamics of diminishing effort, you can mitigate inefficiencies and sustain momentum over the long term.

Presumption of Resistance

Embedded within the fabric of momentum is the presumption of resistance - the recognition that progress is often met with opposition. This resistance can come in the form of internal barriers, such as self-doubt or lack of understanding. These factors are mostly within your power to address. External challenges, such as societal changes, market variations, or institutional constraints, are generally outside of your control. It is up to you to confront these conditions and make the necessary adjustments, or they will diminish the momentum you have gained, and more effort will be required to bring you back to the desired levels of productivity.

In space, a rocket maintains its velocity without continually burning fuel due to the absence of atmospheric drag and other resistive forces. Once a rocket reaches the desired speed, Newton's First Law of Motion - stating that an object in motion stays in motion unless acted upon by an external force - comes into play. Consequently, the rocket continues to move at a constant velocity through the vacuum of space, requiring no additional propulsion to sustain its speed.

However, resistance should not always be viewed as a hindrance. When addressed correctly, it can be a catalyst for adjustment and durability. Using careful planning and calculations, the people who plan space travel regularly employ the gravitational fields of celestial bodies to adjust course.

In overcoming or using resistance, you will develop perseverance, adaptability, and resourcefulness, qualities essential for sustaining momentum in the face of adversity. By reframing resistance as an opportunity for improvement, you can harvest its transformative potential and use momentum to propel you toward your ultimate purpose.

Optimizing Effort and Maximizing Momentum

Navigating the inverse relationship between effort and momentum requires a nuanced understanding of the dynamics at play. Rather than solely focusing on exerting effort, individuals and organizations must utilize strategic interventions that leverage momentum to their advantage. This entails identifying critical inflection points where momentum can be harnessed and capitalized upon, as well as recognizing where to step back and allow momentum to carry you forward autonomously.

As mentioned before, music is a favorite hobby of mine. I have spent many hours in recording studios working on various projects. The most tedious part of the process is the mix-down as it is the phase where volumes, tones and effects are adjusted among many other minute adjustments. In the days of analog (yes I am that old) these adjustments had to be made manually. To speed up the process, the mix-down would take place after all the tracks for all the songs had been recorded. This was done so that settings for tone and effects and a thousand other adjustments could be applied across all the songs so there was consistency in the final product. Now that we have digital recording, these settings can be memorized on the computer and be applied with the touch of a button. This saves a lot of time and effort and sets a working momentum for the process.

By optimizing effort and maximizing momentum, you can achieve greater efficiency, productivity, and impact. Strategic alignment of actions with the trajectory of momentum ensures your efforts are channeled towards meaningful outcomes, while careful allocation of resources minimizes waste and maximizes returns. Embracing the inverse proportionality between effort and momentum unlocks the potential for transformative change and propels you forward to a future of unprecedented opportunities. The point of balance between effort expended and desired momentum is where you will find your sweet spot.

Personal Challenge

Identify and adjust your momentum in various areas of your life by doing the following.

1. **Identify Patterns of Progress**

    Pay attention to recurring successes or positive changes in your life, whether in personal goals, relationships, or work. Recognizing these patterns helps you understand what drives your progress, allowing you to replicate and build on these actions to maintain momentum.

2. **Set Clear, Incremental Goals**

    Break down larger objectives into smaller, manageable tasks. Achieving these smaller milestones generates a sense of accomplishment, reinforcing your momentum and motivating you to continue moving forward.

3. **Assess and Adapt**

    Regularly assess your progress and be willing to adjust your approach. Flexibility allows you to respond to challenges without losing momentum, ensuring you remain on track toward your goals.

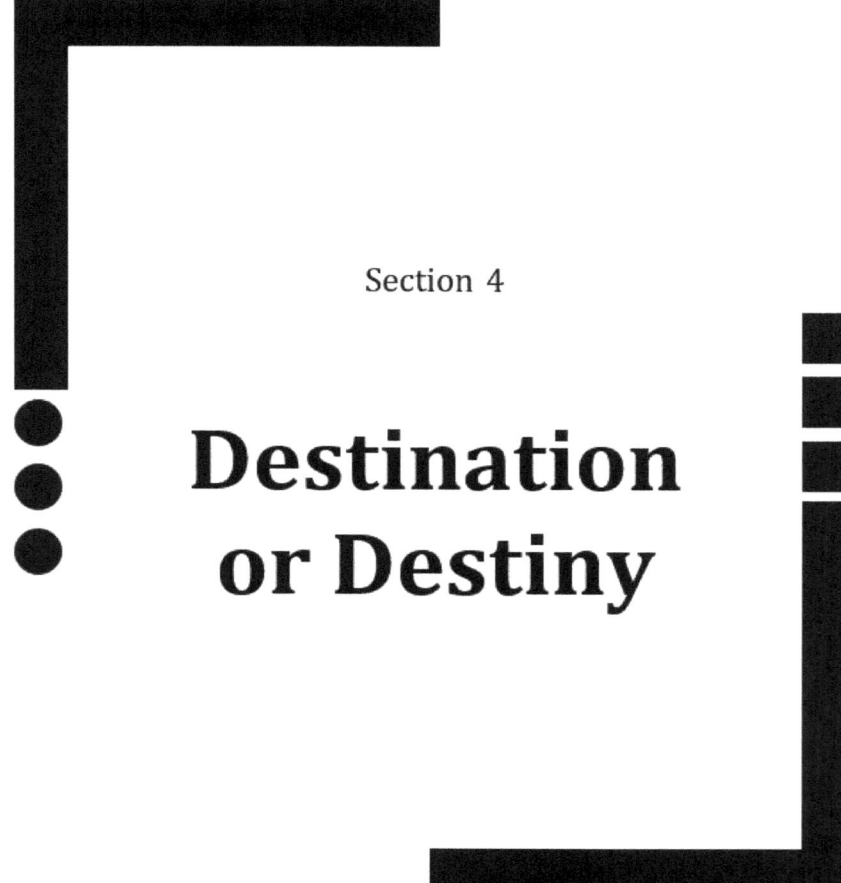

Section 4

Destination
or Destiny

There is a big difference between fulfilling your destiny and settling for a destination in your life trajectory. Destiny entails the realization of your inherent potential and purpose. Destination implies the attainment of a predetermined point, often devoid of deeper meaning or fulfillment. The lives of Neville Chamberlain and Winston Churchill offer compelling illustrations of these contrasting paradigms, exemplifying the consequences of embracing destiny versus acquiescing to mere destinations.

Neville Chamberlain was the British Prime Minister from 1937 to 1940. His political career was marked by a pragmatic approach to governance characterized by a steadfast commitment and desire to avoid conflict at all costs.

In the face of rising tensions in Europe and the specter of Nazi aggression, Chamberlain pursued a policy of diplomatic appeasement, believing that concessions and compromise could avert the looming threat of war. Despite initial successes, such as the Munich Agreement in 1938, this strategy ultimately proved futile in the face of Hitler's unrelenting expansionism.

Chamberlain's name has become synonymous with appeasement and the dangers of settling for expedient solutions rather than confronting underlying challenges. By prioritizing short-term stability over long-term security, he settled for a destination of temporary detente, forsaking the fulfillment of his duty as a defender of liberty and democracy.

In stark contrast to Chamberlain, Winston Churchill was the embodiment of fulfilling destiny through unwavering conviction and strength. Prior to assuming the role of Prime Minister, Churchill's political career was fraught with setbacks and challenges, with his warnings about the growing threat of Nazi Germany often dismissed or ignored.

However, with the outbreak of World War II and Chamberlain's resignation, Churchill found himself thrust into the spotlight as the new leader of Britain. His impassioned rhetoric, steely resolve, and indomitable spirit galvanized the nation in its darkest hour, inspiring fortitude and purpose in the face of adversity.

Churchill's tenure as Prime Minister is etched in history as a testament to his unwavering resolve to fulfilling his destiny as a wartime leader. Despite the immense challenges and sacrifices, Churchill remained steadfast in his pursuit of victory over tyranny.

The lives of Chamberlain and Churchill offer poignant insights into the complexities of navigating destiny and destination. While Chamberlain settled for a destination of temporary peace, Churchill embraced his destiny as a beacon of hope and courage against Hitler's plans for the global expansion of fascism. His sometimes-unpopular approach led Britain and her Allied Forces to victory in World War 2.[45]

On the journey to discover your sweet spot, it's important to have a sense of purpose in your life. Whether it be the right place, wrong time; wrong place, right time; or right place, right time, you must confront the choices that shape your path forward, determining whether you settle for mere destinations or fulfill your true destiny.

---

[45] For a detailed comparison of their policies, consider the following sources.
Parker, R. A. C. (1993). Chamberlain and Appeasement: British Policy and the Coming of the Second World War. New York: Palgrave Macmillan.
Gilbert, Martin (1991). Churchill: A Life. London: Heinemann.
Charmley, John (1993). Churchill: The End of Glory - A Political Biography. New York: Harcourt Brace Jovanovich.

"Follow your bliss, and the universe will open doors where there were only walls."

Joseph Campbell

Author

CHAPTER 15
Fantasy or Purpose

Amidst the many aspirations and fantasies of the human psyche, distinguishing between fleeting whims and genuine desires is essential for living a life of purpose and emotional and spiritual alignment. There is a subtle dichotomy between fantasy and sincere desire. Drawing insights from spiritual and psychological principles helps to illuminate the path while discovering the true desires of your heart.

Transient Possibilities

In my own experience, there are times I would have loved to be a full time musician. While there have been the odd occasion when I got paid for performing or sold a few albums, it has not been more of a fantasy than a practical career choice for me.

Fantasy represents a realm of imagination and possibility, where you imagine idealized scenarios, outcomes, and experiences. They can offer solace and inspiration in times of uncertainty or adversity. When managed correctly, fantasy can indeed provide an occasional escape from the rigors of everyday life. Whether manifested through daydreams, aspirations, or romanticized notions, fantasies hold a seductive allure that captivates the human imagination and beckons toward uncharted horizons.

However, beneath the veneer of fantasy lies a subtle distinction between fleeting whims and enduring desires. While fantasies may provide temporary respite, they often lack the substance, depth, and authenticity that define true desires. True desires emanate from the core of your being, reflecting the deepest longings, values, and aspirations that shape your identity and purpose.

The story of Don Quixote by Miguel de Cervantes[46] illustrates how fantasy can detract from genuine purpose. Quixote enamored with tales of chivalry, embarked on delusional quests, mistaking windmills for giants. His fantasy-driven actions diverted him from meaningful pursuits and harmed those around him. This detachment from reality, spurred by his fantasies, led to misguided efforts and unfulfilled potential. His story underscores the importance of aligning your actions with true purpose as you journey to discover your sweet spot in life.

Discerning, Influencing Factors

Discerning the true desires of the heart requires a process of introspection and emotional and spiritual awareness. It entails delving beneath the surface of whimsical desires and societal expectations to unearth truths that resonate with who you are meant to be.

We live in a world inundated with messages of consumerism, comparison, and instant gratification. If you only pay attention to these messages, you can find yourself, caught in a cycle of chasing after fleeting pleasures and superficial accolades. Yet, true desires emanate from a place of authenticity and alignment with one's core values, beliefs, and convictions. They transcend the fleeting allure of material possessions and societal approval, anchoring you in a deeper sense of meaning and purpose.

Discerning your true desires begins with deep introspection, free from external pressures and expectations. Your passions need to come into alignment with your personal values. Influences like past experiences, significant relationships, and inner conflicts can become either source of help or conflict between who you were and

---

[46] Cervantes Saavedra, Miguel de. Don Quixote. Translated by Edith Grossman, HarperCollins, 2003.

who you are becoming. Reflection and honest self-assessment pave the way to recognizing genuine aspirations and discovering the difference between your destination and destiny.

It would be a beneficial exercise to make a physical list of the things you WANT to do, the things you CAN do and the things you NEED to do. Then beside each item on the list, make a brutally honest assessment of what is fantasy, what is practical reality and what you feel is your true purpose in life. It's important to keen certain fantasies as they can help you escape from time to time.

Embracing Transformation

Discerning true desires involves embracing the power of transformation. It requires a willingness to confront fears, insecurities, and limiting beliefs that obscure your clarity of vision and purpose. Through reflection and spiritual discernment, you can unveil authentic desires that resonate with your unique calling and destiny. As you align your thoughts, words, and actions with the dictates of conscience and conviction, you embark on a journey of discovery and fulfillment.

Maya Angelou experienced such a transformation, leading to the realization of her true purpose. Born in 1928, Angelou faced several hardships early in life, including parental abandonment, racial discrimination, and sexual abuse. These traumatic experiences led to a period of muteness during her childhood, as she struggled to process her pain.

Despite these challenges, Angelou found solace and expression in literature and the arts. Encouraged by her teachers and mentors, she rediscovered her voice and began to channel her experiences into writing and performance. Her memoir, "*I Know Why the Caged*

Bird Sings," published in 1969,[47] brought her international acclaim, and established her as a powerful literary figure. The book's poignant exploration of identity, racism and her ability to overcome it resonated with a wide audience and highlighted the transformative power of storytelling.

Angelou's purpose extended beyond her literary achievements. She became an influential civil rights activist, working alongside leaders like Martin Luther King Jr. and Malcolm X. Her eloquence and insight into the human condition made her a sought-after speaker and an inspiring figure for many. Her transformation from a voiceless child to a renowned author and activist underscores how personal adversity can be a catalyst for discovering one's true destiny and impact countless lives.

Perseverance

Perseverance is the driving force that propels you through life's most challenging moments, revealing your true purpose along the way. It's the quiet strength that keeps you moving forward when everything else urges you to give up. Challenges are inevitable, and they often seem insurmountable, testing your resolve and resilience. Yet, it is through these very challenges that you discover who you truly are. Each obstacle you face provides an opportunity to grow, learn, and redefine your limits.

There is no greater feeling than doing what people say you cannot do. That could well be the tagline of my life. I have been known to stay up late - or all night - to get a task figured out and completed. In fact, whether its physical or mental work, I have to persevere and get the job done. Recently, we decided to repair our lawn so we got to work. We ordered over 5 tons of topsoil and spread it by hand. Then we seeded and leveled and rolled and covered and watered and

---

[47] Angelou, Maya. 1969. I Know Why the Caged Bird Sings. Random House.

at times it felt we would never get tot he end. It took us all day and I lost about 5 pounds just in sweat that day. When I eventually had a shower and sat down, I was so sore, I could barely move. It felt like even my eyelashes were hurting. But the perseverance paid off and soon we were able to look out over a thick, green and level lawn.

When you persevere, you tap into an inner reservoir of strength you may not have known existed. This process of pushing through adversity not only shapes your character but also brings clarity to your life's purpose. The trials you endure force you to confront your deepest fears and insecurities, leading to a greater understanding of yourself and your goals.

In the end, perseverance is about more than just surviving difficulties; it's about thriving in spite of them. It teaches you that your true purpose is not something that is simply handed to you but something that is forged through your struggles. By embracing perseverance, you discover that the path to fulfillment and purpose is often found in the heart of your greatest challenges.

Conclusion

The quest to discern the real desires of the heart is a profound journey. Amidst the chatter of competing voices and conflicting desires that compete for attention, it is incumbent upon you to develop discernment and authenticity in the pursuit of true fulfillment. As you do this, you can navigate the labyrinth of life with clarity, purpose, and integrity. Your sweet spot lies not in the pursuit of passing fantasies, but in alignment, with the fundamental truths that resonate in the depths of your being.

Personal Challenge

Three key factors to help the discovery of your destiny include self-awareness, external influences, and perseverance.

1. Look for ways to understand your strengths, weaknesses, passions, and values, providing clarity on what paths align with your true self.

2. Be aware of how external influences, such as family, culture, mentors, and societal expectations, can shape your perceptions and opportunities, guiding you toward or away from your destined paths.

3. Perseverance is crucial; encountering obstacles and setbacks is inevitable, but a persistent attitude enables you to overcome challenges and stay committed to your goals.

These factors collectively steer you toward realizing your destiny, blending internal and external dynamics.

"Don't ask yourself what the world needs. Ask yourself what makes you come alive, and go do that, because what the world needs is people who have come alive."

Howard Thurman
Theologian, educator and
Civil Rights Leader

CHAPTER 16
Identify Your Passion

On December 26, 2004, a 9.1 magnitude earthquake struck off the coast of Indonesia and triggered a tsunami that devastated coastlines around the Indian Ocean. The eventual death toll from that event was over 225,000 people.

A few months after that event, I was invited to India to visit the affected areas and to speak to the people in a small coastal village that had lost 150 lives on that fateful day. We traveled for 24 hours by air and were picked up at the airport to drive another eight hours from the airport to the village. When we arrived at the hotel, the power had gone out, so we had to climb five floors and lug our bags with us. My host said he would be back to pick me up in two hours for the first meeting.

By 7 PM, over 1000 people had gathered in a little auditorium designed to seat 300. I spent the next three hours speaking to the crowd and talking to individuals. When we finally got back to the hotel around midnight, one of the members of the team came and asked me how I did it. How can I travel for over thirty-six hours and then, with less than two hours to rest and change, spend three hours talking with people in that hot, crowded room? The simple answer is - PASSION. It is the engine that drives my life and motivates me to do the things that I do.

Passion is the fire that ignites your soul, propelling you towards purpose, meaning, and accomplishment. It speaks to the irrepressible yearning within you; the resolute spirit that refuses to be silenced even in the face of adversity and opposition. To identify your passion is to discover your sweet spot and embrace your full potential with conviction and unwavering resolve.

What Gets You Out of Bed in the Morning?

This simple question serves as a potent litmus test for passion – a barometer of your innermost desires, ambitions, and values. For many, the answer may be rooted in the necessity of work, the imperative of earning a paycheck to meet the demands of daily life. Yet, beneath the surface of obligation, lies the potential for something far greater – a sense of purpose, fulfillment, and joy that transcends the confines of mere survival.

Indeed, the pursuit of passion is not merely a luxury reserved for the fortunate few, but the birthright inherent in human existence. It is the energy that animates your being, infusing each moment with vitality, meaning, and significance.

Whether expressed through creativity, inquiry, or service to others, passion embodies the essence of your true self. It gets you out of bed and carries you through the day, even when circumstances are adverse. It motivates you long after the doors are closed and the lights are turned off.

Taking the Lead

The question then arises: can you give yourself 100% to your passion? Can you wholeheartedly commit yourself to the pursuit of that which sets your soul ablaze, regardless of the obstacles, challenges, or sacrifices that may lie ahead? The answer lies in the depths of your own heart, where the true measure of your commitment resides.

Brett Favre's[48] passion for football profoundly shaped his life and career. From an early age, Favre demonstrated an exceptional talent and love for the game, leading him to excel in high school and

---

[48] Pearlman, Jeff. 2016. Gunslinger: The Remarkable, Improbable, Iconic Life of Brett Favre. Houghton Mifflin Harcourt.

college football. His dedication and skill earned him a place in the NFL, where he became the starting quarterback for the Green Bay Packers.

Favre's relentless work ethic and enthusiasm for football resulted in an illustrious 20-year career. He set several records, including being the first NFL player to throw five hundred touchdown passes and amassing over 70,000 passing yards. Favre's leadership and on-field charisma endeared him to fans and teammates alike, making him one of the most iconic figures in football history.

Off the field, Favre's passion for the game inspired his philanthropic efforts, including a Foundation which supports disadvantaged and disabled children. His commitment to football not only defined his professional success but also enabled him to make a positive impact on his community, demonstrating how passion can drive both personal and societal achievements.

For some, the pursuit of passion may require a leap of faith – a willingness to relinquish the safety and security of the familiar in favor of the unknown and uncertain. It may demand perseverance in the face of setbacks, determination in the face of rejection, and resolve in the face of doubt and despair. Yet, it is precisely in moments of adversity and opposition that the flame of passion burns brightest, illuminating the path forward with clarity and purpose.

Transcendence

The pursuit of passion transcends the boundaries of material gain or external recognition. It is not contingent upon the promise of wealth, fame, or success, but rooted in the intrinsic value of the journey itself – the joy of creation, the fulfillment of service, and the boundless potential of the human spirit. Whether expressed through art, music, science, or philanthropy, passion emanates from the depths of your being, radiating out with transformative power and grace.

As a kid, I lived in Calcutta, India - now known as Kolkata. Less than 0.3 miles (0.5 km) from where we lived was the home of a little nun. All we knew of her at the time was that she took care of people that most respectable Indians would not go near. It was not until after we left India in 1972 that we began to appreciate the scope of her work.

Mother Teresa's selfless passion for serving the poor and destitute defined her life's mission. Born Anjeze Gonxhe Bojaxhiu in 1910 in Macedonia, she dedicated her life to helping the needy. In 1950, she founded the Missionaries of Charity in Calcutta, focusing on aiding the sick, orphaned, and dying. Her unwavering compassion and humility drove her to work tirelessly in some of the world's most impoverished areas. Awarded the Nobel Peace Prize in 1979, Mother Teresa's legacy is a testament to the profound impact of selfless love and dedication to humanity, inspiring countless others through her passionate service.[49]

Indeed, the true test of passion lies not in the pursuit of self-interest but in the service of something greater than yourself. It is the willingness to sacrifice, to endure, and to persevere, fueled by a sense of purpose and integrity, that transcends ego and ambition. It is the willingness to stand firm in your convictions, to speak truth to power, and to embody the values that inspire, uplift, and unite us as human beings.

Paying the Price

Would you do it for no pay? This question cuts to the heart of passion, challenging you to examine the intrinsic value of your

---

[49] Spink, Kathryn. 2011. Mother Teresa: An Authorized Biography. Harper One.

pursuits beyond the realm of material reward or external validation. It invites you to consider whether your passion embodies the essence of your deepest values, aspirations, and ideals. Passion is not simply a transactional exchange or an internal motivation. It is that covenantal – some would say spiritual – sweet spot between the reason for your existence and living your purpose.

Would you give up what you previously settled for to attain what is deep in your being? This final question serves as the ultimate litmus test for passion – a testament to the depths of your commitment and the strength of your convictions. It challenges you to confront your deepest fears, to transcend your limitations, and to embrace the fullness of your potential with courage, grace, and unwavering resolve. For passion is not merely a fleeting emotion, or passing fantasy, but a sacred calling to live, to love, and to serve with everything that resides within you.

Conclusion

Living in your passion is crucial because it aligns your work with your core values, leading to a more fulfilling and purposeful life. When you operate from this place, you experience greater motivation and creativity, allowing you to face and overcome challenges more easily. Passion fuels your purpose, guiding you with energy and enthusiasm. It also enhances your well-being, as doing what you love brings a sense of joy and satisfaction. Ultimately, living in the sweet spot of your passion empowers you to make a more significant impact in your personal and professional life.

Personal Challenge

If you are still not sure what your passion is, ask and answer these questions.

1. What really gets you out of bed in the morning?

2. Can you give yourself wholeheartedly to it?

3. Are you prepared to lay aside the things that stand in the way of fulfilling your passion?

When you can answer these questions honestly, you will have not only identified your passion, but you are also well on your way to finding and living in your sweet spot.

"Authenticity is the daily practice of letting go of who we think we're supposed to be and embracing who we are."

Bené Brown

Professor and Author

CHAPTER 17
Embracing Authenticity

Every person on this earth has some inherent abilities or personality traits, regardless of physical or mental capacity. It may be leadership, compassion, generosity, service, unusual insight, or several other qualities. It is a pity that few people can match these inherent qualities with their vocation or life's work.

Often, these traits are interpreted through the lens of personality types. While personality type assessments are a handy tool, the resulting classifications can be colored by your current circumstances, physical and especially your emotional state at the time. There are a variety of tests available, and some are much better than others. I have listed a few suggestions in the resource's appendix.

The point is that discovering your natural abilities and propensities does not have to be a struggle. For example, a person may love music but does not comprehend the technicalities and disciplines of study and practice that are involved in becoming a top-class musician. (Wait. Maybe I am thinking about myself).

What I am getting at is that your love for music may be a great hobby, but your aptitude for numbers and formulas may make you more suited to a career in mathematics or science. I went to school with a person who was a math genius and was able to comprehend complex math concepts. At the age of fourteen, he actually coached one of his math teachers through her Master's degree studies.

Having good mentoring relationships is key to discovering what these natural propensities are at an early age. Parents, don't drive your children to what you think would be a prosperous career for them. Guide them – get help if necessary – to discover early on what they are good at and enjoy. I love and live by the adage, if you love what you do, you will never have to work a day in your life.

Resonance

Doing what flows naturally means aligning your actions and aspirations with the inherent gifts and passions that resonate within the depths of your being. It involves embracing the unique expression of individuality that distinguishes each person's contribution to the world. Just as a square peg does not fit into a round hole, attempting to conform to societal expectations or emulate the pursuits of others may lead to a sense of dissonance and unfulfillment.

I spent years trying to follow a path that I thought involved meeting the needs of everyone who came to me with anything. Even after my physical challenges in 2015, I made some adjustments to my lifestyle and the way I approached my work but I found myself drawn back into responding to every need. It wasn't until I flirted with burning out and I started exploring creative outlets—writing, speaking, etc.—even exploring nice ways to say no to some things - that I realized my true sweet spot and became far more effective at helping others discover their potential.

Discerning between natural inclination and momentary impulses is essential in helping you find your sweet spot. Impulsiveness is the tendency to act on whims without forethought. While acting on impulse can bring excitement and spontaneity, it can often lead to risky decisions with unintended consequences.

What you want to achieve is a resonance – a sweet spot – between your desires, abilities, and opportunities. Resonance is not automatic or even easy but occurs when you embrace who you are created to be, free from manipulation. As I found out the hard way, it empowers you to thrive with integrity and purpose, forming genuine connections with the people that need you the most.

Emulate or Create

The pursuit and realization of authenticity necessitates resisting the temptation to emulate others. While emulation may offer temporary gratification or validation, it leads to a sense of inauthenticity and stagnation in realizing your destiny. Instead of constantly seeking external recognition, or comparing yourself to others, pursue the expression of your gifts and talents, celebrating the creativity and uniqueness of your design.

For example, in music, each musician possesses a distinct feel, groove, and expression that reflects their unique personality, experiences, and influences. Attempting to mimic or replicate the style of others may dilute one's true talent and hinder the full expression of their creative potential. Instead, musicians are encouraged to find their own voice, explore their unique sound, and honor the creative impulses that flow naturally from within.

Here are seven ways to boost creativity in an authentic way.

1. Incorporate Curiosity. Encourage questioning and curiosity. Explore new ideas, ask "what if" questions, and remain open to new experiences and perspectives. This can spark innovative thinking and lead to creative solutions.

2. Create a Stimulating Environment. Surround yourself with diverse stimuli, such as art, music, books, and nature. A stimulating environment can inspire new ideas and creative connections.

3. Collaborate with Others. Engage in discussions and collaborations with people from different backgrounds and

fields. Diverse perspectives can challenge your thinking and lead to unique, creative outcomes.

4. Take Breaks and Relax. Step away from work to rest and recharge. Activities like walking, meditating, or engaging in a hobby can clear your mind and allow subconscious ideas to surface.

5. Understand your Calling. Creativity is not simply a way to make money or a name for yourself. The unique mix that makes you also defines your calling and gives you the ability to be creative. Becoming aware of this reduces the stress of having to compete, creating mental space for creativity to flourish.

6. Set Aside Time for Creative Thinking. Dedicate specific time for brainstorming and creative activities. Regular musing reinforces creative habits and provides opportunities for innovative ideas to emerge.

7. Embrace Failure and Experimentation. View failures as learning opportunities. Experiment with new ideas without fear of failure, as this willingness to take risks can lead to unexpected and innovative solutions.

Level Playing Field

The concept of a level playing field became popular in the early 1980's. It is appealing in many ways, but it fails to account for the unique characteristics and passions that exist in humanity. Since gaining popularity, this concept has become overused to the point of jargon for the concept of "fair competition without inherent advantage for any party."[50]

---

[50] Deccan Herald, January 9, 2008 - India's 61st Cavalry rides into 56th year

Michael Phelps is unique due to his extraordinary swimming abilities. His achievements include a record 23 Olympic gold medals in five consecutive Olympic Games from 2000 to 2016, setting many world records along the way. His physical build, unparalleled work ethic, versatility across multiple events, and ability to perform under pressure have cemented his status as one of the greatest athletes in history. I could never swim like Phelps, but then, he has never achieved some of the things I have.

The point is, while we may share some similarities with others, we are all unique. From our physical make-up to our emotional and mental disposition to our environment, we all have traits and abilities that set us apart from other people. When you base your life on the comparative advantages or disadvantages of others, you are living in their sweet spot, not yours. There is a better way to live. Embrace the authentic you.

Conclusion

The importance of doing what flows naturally underscores the value of authenticity, discernment, and alignment with your purpose in life. By recognizing the difference between natural inclination and aberrant impulses, you can embrace originality and creativity, and live a life of purpose, fulfillment, and integrity.

Personal Challenge

Here are some suggestions to help get you started. Some are covered in a little more depth in other chapters. The more you do it, the more instinctive it becomes.

1. **Assessment**

   Conduct a thorough self-assessment to understand your strengths, weaknesses, passions, and goals. Then, get someone you know well and trust to do the same assessment and see how close the results line up. This clarity helps in identifying opportunities that align with your abilities and desires.

2. **Networking and Mentorship**

   Build a strong network and seek guidance from mentors. They can provide valuable insights, advice, and connections that open doors to opportunities aligned with your desires and abilities. These networks are not just for you to receive something for yourself. It is also a good place to evaluate how others receive input from you.

3. **Proactive Exploration**

   Actively seek and explore opportunities. This involves researching, attending events, and staying informed about trends in your areas of interest to find the best matches for your aspirations and skill set.

"Without good direction, people lose their way; the more wise counsel you follow, the better your chances."

Proverbs 11:14

The Message Translation

CHAPTER 18
Getting Help

As a minister in my early 30s, I was helping a young man deal with some personal issues in his life. The more we talked, the more I realized that I was out of my depth. My middle-class, safe family upbringing did not give me any frame of reference for what I was hearing from him. Eventually, I was able to track down someone who was a specialist in the areas in which this man needed help. Initially, I felt like I might have let him down, but over the years, I have come to know the value of knowing my limitations and seeking help when I am not in my sweet spot.

The profound, enduring wisdom of the Bible, underscores the importance of seeking counsel and guidance from those who possess greater maturity and experience in specific areas of life. To put it bluntly, it has saved my bacon on a few occasions. In the pursuit of personal growth, decision-making, and finding your sweet spot, the act of seeking counsel emerges as a transformative practice that empowers you to navigate challenges, get wisdom, and resolve to find and live in your destiny.

Knowing Your Limits

Let us begin by recognizing that human wisdom is limited, and the journey of life is fraught with some challenges that will mostly not be resolved by chance. In times of crisis or adversity, you will benefit immensely from the perspective, insight, and guidance offered by trusted advisers. Whether navigating career transitions, relational, conflict, or moral dilemmas, seeking counsel provides a valuable opportunity to gain clarity, discernment, and direction amidst the ebb and flow of life.

Knowing your limits offers several benefits that enhance both personal well-being and professional performance. Perhaps the most important benefit is it helps prevent burnout by allowing you to manage your energy and avoid over-commitment. Recognizing your boundaries enables you to prioritize tasks effectively, focusing on what truly matters and delegating or declining activities that exceed your capacity. This awareness promotes better decision-making, as you can assess situations realistically and set achievable goals.

I can tell you from personal experience that recognizing the thresholds of your abilities promotes a healthier work-life balance, reducing stress and improving overall mental and physical health. It also enhances your ability to communicate your needs and set boundaries with others, leading to more respectful and productive relationships. In a professional context, knowing your limits allows you to seek help and collaborate effectively, leveraging the strengths of others to achieve common goals.

This empowers sustainable growth, eventually pushing your boundaries without compromising your well-being or effectiveness.

The Benefits of Experience

Expert counsel is better than peer affirmation because it provides experienced, informed, and objective guidance tailored to your specific situation. Experts possess specialized knowledge and skills that can help you navigate complex challenges, make sound decisions, and avoid potential pitfalls. While peer affirmation offers emotional support, it may lack the depth and accuracy needed for critical decision-making. Relying on expert counsel ensures you receive reliable advice that can lead to more successful outcomes.

Seeking counsel from those who possess greater maturity or experience in specific areas of life amplifies the value and relevance of the guidance received. Just as a novice seeks the instruction of a seasoned mentor, you can benefit from the wisdom and perspective offered by those who have negotiated similar paths and weathered comparable storms. Whether seeking career advice, marital counseling, or spiritual guidance, turning to mentors, or experts in the field facilitates informed decision-making and growth.

I have had the same family doctor for over 15 years. He is softly spoken, doesn't use medical jargon when explaining things to me and takes an interest in the back story of my life as he advises on a course of action. Even when he needs to correct a preconceived or wrong understanding, he does it without making me feel like I'm a fool for not knowing what he knows.

The quality of counsel received is profoundly affected by the character and disposition of the counselor. Positive, affirming, and encouraging counselors uplift and inspire you, instilling confidence, hope, and a way forward in the face of adversity. Their words and actions nurture a sense of empowerment and affirmation and build an environment conducive to growth, healing, and transformation.

Yes, You Can

Negative or pessimistic counselors undermine confidence, sow seeds of doubt, and perpetuate a cycle of cynicism and despair. Their toxic disposition erodes trust, stifles creativity, and impedes progress, relegating you to a state of resignation and defeat. By surrounding yourself with positive influences and cultivating relationships that uplift and inspire, you create a generative space for personal and professional growth.

For example, the caution against seeking counsel for financial matters from "broke" people underscores the importance of discernment and wisdom in choosing advisers. Financial decisions carry profound implications for your well-being, security, and future prosperity. Seeking guidance from people who lack financial literacy or discipline may lead to misguided advice and adverse outcomes. Instead, you do well when you seek counsel from financial advisors, mentors, or experts who possess a history of good stewardship, integrity, and success.

Conclusion

The admonition to seek counsel, as articulated in Proverbs 11:14, resonates with enduring consequence and wisdom. It requires a willingness to acknowledge your limitations, biases, and blind spots, recognizing that the wisdom and experience of others can shed light on areas of darkness or confusion that you might miss yourself. By embracing humility, vulnerability, and being open to receiving guidance, you set yourself up for a transformative journey of growth and empowerment.

Through the guidance of trusted counselors and advisers, you will also gain clarity and direction when navigating life's complexities. By surrounding yourself with positive influences and exercising discernment in choosing advisers, you nurture a culture of purpose and growth that resonates with finding and living in your sweet spot.

Personal Challenge

Choosing the right advisors is crucial for success in any endeavor, whether it's a business project or a personal goal. Here are three key points to consider:

1. **Expertise and Experience**

   Select advisors who have a deep understanding of the specific area in which you need guidance. They should have a proven track record of success in relevant fields, bringing valuable insights and practical advice. Their experience should align with your purpose and challenges.

2. **Values Alignment**

   It is important to choose advisors who share similar values and understand your vision. This ensures that their advice will be consistent with your overall strategy and objectives. A good cultural fit also facilitates better communication and collaboration, making it easier to work together effectively.

3. **Network and Resources**

   Advisors should bring more than just knowledge - they should also have a strong network and access to resources that can benefit you. Whether it is industry connections, access to capital, or knowledge of new opportunities, an advisor with a robust network can open doors and provide additional support beyond their direct advice.

"Quality without results is pointless. Results without quality is boring."

Johan Cruyff

Dutch Footballer

CHAPTER 19
Producing Good Results

I lay there in the emergency room, listening to an alarm go off every few minutes as my blood pressure kept rising. When I first came in, my blood pressure was 217/105. They gave me something to bring it down and thought it would work quickly. Over the next five hours, my blood pressure kept creeping up. Eventually, they decided to keep me in overnight and bring it down slowly. Twenty hours later, my blood pressure was down to a more manageable level, and so they released me on the provision that I go see my family doctor immediately.

As my doctor looked through my records, he told me that I would need to give up some of my activities as I was doing too much and that was the main contributor to my hypertension. Over the next few weeks, I made some changes and gave up some things that were causing me stress. Two months later, my blood pressure was back down to the normal range. Interestingly, I was as busy as ever, only now I was busy doing the things that were producing good results in my life because I was back in my sweet spot.

Any farmer will tell you there is no point in sowing seeds in a field if there is no expectation of a harvest. In anticipation of good results, there are several factors that go into planting seeds and tending the growth to maximize the crop. Organizing, preparing, sowing, watering, and fertilizing are a few factors that help achieve the intended results.

Farmers that omit any of these essential functions suffer the consequences. So it is with your life. Finding and living in your sweet spot not only brings a sense of purpose, it will also produce good results.

Cut off the Dead Wood

"Don't waste time on things that don't work." This caution serves as a reminder of the importance of sound judgment in the pursuit of our goals and aspirations. In the constant distractions and competing priorities of life, it is all too easy to squander our precious time and energy on endeavors that yield little or no lasting value. Yet, true fulfillment lies not in the accumulation of experiences, but in zeroing in on the most productive experiences that will improve our results.

Much like I had to prune my activities to manage my blood pressure, there comes a time when we must decide which areas of our life are truly producing the best results. Pruning is a vital part of the process, a necessary step in the journey of growth and productivity. Just as skilled gardeners prune the branches of a plant or tree to promote healthy growth and abundant fruitfulness, so too we must undergo periods of cutting back on certain things in our own lives. These may take the form of challenges, setbacks, or trials, which test our resolve, refine our character, and deepen our sense of purpose. Far from being a punishment or a sign of failure, pruning is an act of self-discipline that strengthens and empowers us to bear more fruit in a sustainable and more prolific manner.

Nixing Nostalgia

Nostalgia is one of the beautiful human qualities that can bring back memories and emotions of wonderful times long past. But when unchecked, nostalgia can be the enemy of fruitfulness – a subtle trap that ensnares you in a web of the past, preventing you from fully embracing the opportunities that await you in the present.

On a recent trip to Australia to see our families, we drove or walked by a few places that represented some very pleasant times from early in our marriage. Sunday afternoons on the beach with other recently married couples, our first apartment where there were many laughter filled evenings as we played Connect Four with an intensity that would rival the highest levels of chess tournaments and other personal and professional landmarks in our journey. The nostalgia evoked a momentary yearning for those simpler and fun filled times but I know I could never have achieved what I have so far if I was to stay limited to the experiences back then.

While it is natural to cherish fond memories and reflect on past experiences - indeed it could prove beneficial to repeat a few of the things that were productive - clinging to nostalgia can blind you to what is right in front of you. It can shackle you to the ghosts of the past, preventing you from fully embracing the new beginning and fresh opportunities that beckon just on the horizon.

Henry Ford introduced the assembly line in 1913.[51] It absolutely revolutionized and improved the efficiency of automobile production, reducing the time it took to assemble a car from over 12 hours to about 1.5 hours. Since that time, the assembly line has been improved in countless ways to speed up the process even more. In many areas, the introduction of robotics has significantly increased the quality, accuracy, and efficiency of production while reducing waste and increasing safety. If we were to hold on to Ford's original idea and ways of running the assembly line for the sake of nostalgia, the automobile industry would never keep up with the demands of the modern world.

Patience and Good Judgment

In the pursuit of good results, it is important to nurture qualities, such as patience, perseverance, and humility – virtues that enable

---

[51] "Ford's Assembly Line." Henry Ford Museum of American Innovation, The Henry Ford, www.thehenryford.org/collections-and-research/digital-collections/artifact/216402

you to weather life's storms with grace and courage. As mentioned in an earlier chapter, the journey to overnight success can be a long and challenging one. Good and lasting results can take time.

Thomas Edison's 10,000 attempts to create a functional light bulb exemplify patience, determination, and innovation.[52] Despite many failures, Edison viewed each attempt as a step closer to success, famously stating that he had not failed but rather discovered 10,000 ways that did not work. This relentless experimentation and unwavering determination eventually led to the invention of a practical and long-lasting electric light bulb in 1879. Edison's journey underscores the importance of persistence in achieving progress. He was ultimately able to transform the lighting industry and modern life through patience and sound judgment.

Build relationships that uplift, inspire, and empower you to become the best version of yourself and draw others along with you. True fruitfulness lies not in isolation or hoarding your increase to yourself. Often including others in the process, increases the quality and profitability of the final product.

Engage Technology

Engaging technology to improve productivity offers several benefits. It streamlines workflows by automating repetitive tasks, freeing up time for more nuanced activities. Tools like project management software enhance organization, ensuring deadlines are met, and projects stay on track. Collaboration platforms facilitate real-time communication, promoting teamwork and reducing delays. Data analytics tools provide insights into performance, helping to identify inefficiencies and optimize processes. Remote

[52] "Thomas Edison's 10,000 Attempts to Create the Lightbulb." Thomas Edison National Historical Park, National Park Service, www.nps.gov/edis/learn/historyculture/thomas-edison-and-the-light-bulb.htm

work technology enables flexibility, allowing teams to work efficiently from anywhere. Overall, leveraging technology increases efficiency, reduces errors, enhances collaboration, and provides valuable insights, leading to higher productivity and better business outcomes.

The work output of those that know how to harness the power of technology is far superior to those that still refuse to embrace it. While watching a master carpenter at work is awe-inspiring, it is not a good method of mass production. Examine the benefits of automation, artificial intelligence, social media, or hundreds of other technology tools that can help improve the volume and quality of your output.

Teamwork

Teamwork also enhances motivation and productivity, with members supporting and encouraging each other towards common goals. Effective communication and coordination within a team ensure that tasks are completed efficiently and to a high standard. The power of teamwork lies in its ability to combine efforts, leading to superior outcomes that surpass individual capabilities.

Key partnerships are crucial in increasing productivity. For example, the highest efficiency air-conditioning unit may be a useful product, but you will not sell a lot of inventory in the Arctic Circle. If you could find a partner in the tropics, where air conditioning is in high demand, you would have discovered a sweet spot. When you add in manufacturing, shipping, and service partnerships, you have grown your sweet spot and increased the power of production for your endeavor.

Teamwork harnesses the collective strengths and diverse skills of individuals to achieve outstanding results. By working together, team members can tackle complex problems more effectively, leveraging each person's unique expertise and perspective. This synergy advances creativity and innovation, as ideas are shared and refined collaboratively.

Conclusion

The pursuit of good fruit is not merely a task or obligation. The goal is a calling that embodies the highest ideals and objectives of your destiny. It is a journey of growth, transformation, and renewal – a journey that invites us to align our thoughts, words, and actions in a way that will help us realize the ultimate purpose for which we are placed in this life. Learn and practice the discipline of pruning away the things that no longer serve you or are a negative influence as you function in your destiny. Engage all the tools at your disposal so you can become the most productive that you can be.

Don't settle for a destination. Keep moving till you find the sweet spot of your destiny.

Personal Challenge

Evaluating productivity effectively requires a comprehensive approach that considers both quantitative and qualitative factors. Here are three key points to consider:

1. **Output Measurement**

    The most direct way to evaluate productivity is by measuring the output relative to the input. This could involve assessing the quantity and quality of work produced within a specific timeframe, such as units produced, tasks completed, or services delivered. Comparing this output to the resources used (e.g., time, labor, materials) helps determine efficiency.

2. **Goal Alignment and Achievement**

    Productivity should also be evaluated based on how well work contributes to overall goals. This involves assessing whether the tasks being completed are driving progress toward key objectives. High productivity means not just doing more but doing more of what matters most for success.

3. **Consistency and Improvement**

    Evaluate productivity over time to see if there is consistency in performance and a trend of improvement. Productivity isn't just about short-term bursts of efficiency but maintaining and increasing it in the long run. This includes looking at whether employees or systems are becoming more efficient and effective, reducing waste, or enhancing processes over time.

Section 5

Maximizing Your Sweet Spot

The concept of the sweet spot is about aligning your work and life with what you love, what you are good at, and what the world needs. At this point in your reading, I hope you have thought about some things and, if you have not worked them out, are at least well on your way to doing so.

Your sweet spot lies at the intersection of four primary areas.

1. Passions: What gets you out of bed?

2. Strengths: What you do well?

3. Job: What pays the bills?

4. Opportunities: What is available?

©2024 Ian Peters/Cityflights Global Leadership

178

When these elements intersect, you are likely to find that space in your life and work that is not only satisfying but is also sustainable and profitable. The more concentric these circles are, the larger your sweet spot will be. From there, it is up to you to decide whether you want to settle for what you have discovered or use that as a steppingstone to grow and reach greater heights.

If you think about some of the more well-known entrepreneurs in history and those operating currently - Bill Gates, Elon Musk, Steve Jobs, etc. - you will see that they did not stop because they had attained a measure of success. They continued to build on that success till they had maximized what they felt their lives were meant to be about.

Working within your sweet spot ensures that you are engaged in activities that you find inherently rewarding. This intrinsic motivation leads to greater job satisfaction and a sense of purpose. When your work aligns with your strengths, you are more likely to excel. Your ability translates into higher quality output and efficiency, which are critical for life career advancement and recognition. Take steps to ensure that your skills remain relevant and in demand. This not only enhances job stability but also opens opportunities for growth and advancement.

A strong alignment of these areas makes you better equipped to adapt to changes and persist through difficulties, as your work resonates with your core interests and abilities. Operating within your sweet spot allows you to contribute meaningfully to your field or community. Your unique combination of skills and passions can drive innovation and create value that extends beyond personal gain.

"Setting goals is the first step in turning the invisible to the visible."

Anthony Robbins

Motivational Speaker

CHAPTER 20
Set Clear Goals

Setting clear goals is foundational towards achieving success and maximizing productivity in any endeavor. Whether you are working on a project, pursuing a personal passion, or striving to reach professional milestones, having well-defined objectives provides a roadmap for your efforts and ensures you stay focused on what truly matters.

Guideposts

Clear goals serve as the guiding principles that steer your actions and decisions toward anticipated outcomes. They provide a sense of direction, clarity, and purpose, empowering you to prioritize tasks, allocate resources systematically, and measure progress effectively. Without clear goals, you risk wandering aimlessly, expending energy and resources on activities that may not align with your main objectives.

Clear goals enhance motivation and commitment by offering tangible markers to strive for. When you have a clear understanding of what youare working towards and why it matters, youare more likely to stay on purpose and press on in the face of challenges. In addition, clear goals facilitate productive partnerships, ensuring that all stakeholders are aligned and working towards a common objective.

S. M. A. R. T.

It has been around for a while, but there is a tried and proven acronym that helps when setting goals in any area of life. S. M. A.

R. T.[53] This stands for Specific, Measurable, Achievable, Relevant, and Time-bound. Letus briefly break down each component.

Specific. Clearly define what you aim to achieve, avoiding vague or ambiguous language. Be specific about the desired outcome, the actions required to achieve it, and the resources available to support your efforts.

Measurable. Establish concrete metrics or milestones to track progress and gauge success. Measurable goals provide a clear indication of whether youare on track or need to adjust your strategies.

Achievable. Set goals that are challenging yet attainable, considering your skills, resources, and constraints. Know the difference between informed practicality and fantasy, which may lead to frustration or burnout. Break down larger goals into smaller, manageable tasks to maintain momentum and build confidence.

Relevant. Ensure that your goals are aligned with your broader objectives and purpose. Consider the impact of your goals on yourself, your family, your organization, and other stakeholders. Focus on activities that will contribute to long-term success.

Time-bound. Set deadlines or timelines to create a sense of urgency and accountability. Clearly define start and end dates for each goal, breaking down larger projects into smaller, time-bound milestones. This helps prevent procrastination and ensures that you make steady progress towards your objectives.

---

[53]There's a S.M.A.R.T. Way to Write Management's Goals and Objectives.
©1981. George T. Doran. Management Review, Vol. 70, Issue 11, pp. 35-36.

When I was first invited to present my ideas for this book, there were a number of things that had to be done. I had to gather my resources and put them together in a way that would make my point. It had to fit in with the other work that I was committed to at the time. Six months was the period I allotted myself, and set some minor goals along the way. At the time of writing this very sentence, I was ahead of my original schedule by about a week.

When I realized I was a week ahead of schedule, it felt like all the planning and late nights were finally paying off. I could almost hear a small voice saying, 'This is why you set clear goals in the first place.' It's moments like these that remind you of the power of focus.

Enhanced Results

Setting clear goals offers several benefits that enhance productivity and performance. You are not just looking for a result; you are looking for the best result.

1. Focus. Clear goals keep your sweet spot in the picture, helping you prioritize tasks and allocate resources. They enable you to concentrate your energy on activities that move you closer to your objectives, reducing distractions and increasing efficiency.

2. Motivation. Well-defined goals serve as powerful motivators, inspiring you to act in the face of difficulties. When you have a clear vision of how to work in your sweet spot and why it matters, youare more likely to stay motivated and energized.

3. Clarity. Clear goals define a tangible direction, reducing doubt and confusion about what needs to be done. They provide a vector for your efforts, guiding decision-making

and ensuring that everyone involved is aligned and working towards a common purpose.

4. Accountability. Clear goals build accountability by establishing detailed expectations for your actions. Specificity makes you more likely to hold yourself accountable for your progress and take ownership of your outcomes.

In 1961, President John F. Kennedy set a clear and ambitious goal for the United States: to land a man on the Moon and return him safely to Earth before the decade's end.[54] This goal provided a focused direction and galvanized efforts across various sectors, including government, industry, and academia. The clear objective led to the development of new technologies, rigorous planning, and meticulous project management. As a result, on July 20, 1969, NASA successfully landed astronauts Neil Armstrong and Buzz Aldrin on the Moon during the Apollo 11 mission.

I was nine years old and still living in India at the time. Television had not yet arrived in Calcutta and there was very limited English programming available so we had to listen to Voice of America on shortwave radio to follow the event. I remember it was a Sunday and our family raced home from church so we could listen to the preparation for landing and eventually hear the words, "Houston, Tranquility base here. The Eagle has Landed." (Curiously, as I write this, I notice the date is July 20th, 2024 – 55 years to the day of that historic event).

The clarity of the mission's goal not only united a nation but also accelerated technological advancements and solidified the United

[54] Kennedy, John F. "Special Message to the Congress on Urgent National Needs." Delivered 25 May 1961. The American Presidency Project, University of California, Santa Barbara. https://www.presidency.ucsb.edu/documents/special-message-the-congress-urgent-national-needs.

States' position as a leader in space exploration. The Apollo Program remains a prime example of how setting precise and ambitious goals can drive exceptional achievement.

Conclusion

Goal setting is essential for maximizing productivity, achieving success, and realizing your full potential. By following the SMART criteria, you can create a roadmap for your efforts and ensure that your work product is aligned with your intended outcomes. Clear goals empower you to make steady progress toward your ultimate destiny and achieve extraordinary results in your endeavors to find and live in your sweet spot.

Personal Challenge

1. Set a goal – personal or professional – that you can achieve within a month. Make it challenging but achievable. Use SMART.

2. Make a realistic list of resources, personnel, and steps you need to take to realize that goal.

3. Engage an accountability partner – preferably outside the practical process of realizing your goal. I find this helps the pitfalls of making excuses or procrastinating. Plan a celebration when you are done.

Goal setting and achievement are something you can become better at, simply by doing it again and again. After a while, it becomes almost automatic.

"Education is the most powerful weapon which you can use to change the world."

Nelson Mandela

President, South Africa

CHAPTER 21
Continue Learning

You may have discovered your sweet spot already. Congratulations! But wouldn't it be great if you could maximize that discovery to be even more impactful in your personal and professional life?

Continuing to learn and grow is a cornerstone of personal and professional achievement. In today's rapidly changing world, where new technologies emerge, industries evolve, and knowledge expands at an extraordinary pace, the importance of continuous learning cannot be overstated. Whether youare striving to excel in your career, pursue your passions, or simply stay abreast of innovations in your field, a commitment to systematic learning is essential for boosting your potential and enhancing the quality of your life and work.

Staying Relevant

Ongoing education is essential for staying relevant, and competitive in today's dynamic marketplace. As technology advances and industries undergo transformation, the skills and knowledge required to succeed, evolve accordingly. By investing in ongoing education, you equip yourself with the tools, insights, and expertise needed to navigate change, seize opportunities, and thrive in your chosen field.

Intellectual curiosity, creativity, and innovation are the driving forces behind progress and breakthroughs. If you want to stay relevant in your field, you must explore current ideas, challenge assumptions, and think critically about the issues. By expanding your horizons and pushing the boundaries of your knowledge, you develop a growth mindset and position yourself as a lifelong learner, keeping abreast of new possibilities and discoveries.

Netflix is a company that stayed relevant through changes in the consumer video industry.[55] Originally a DVD rental service, Netflix anticipated changes in technology and consumer behavior, transitioning to a streaming platform. They invested heavily in data analytics to understand viewer preferences, enabling them to produce popular original content like "House of Cards" and "Stranger Things" – among many others. By constantly adapting its business model, embracing modern technologies, and learning from user data, Netflix maintained its position as a leader in the entertainment industry, successfully navigating the shift from physical media to digital streaming.

Education Options

There are various methods for continuing education, each offering unique benefits and opportunities for growth.

1. Workshops and Seminars. Over the years, I have been the beneficiary of many such events. These days, I am the one speaking or presenting - sometimes to a handful and sometimes to hundreds and I strive to present great value to attendees. Participating in workshops, seminars, and conferences allows you to get away from the normal routine and immerse yourself in focused learning experiences, interact with experts in your field, and gain practical insights and strategies for success. These events often feature presentations, panel discussions, and networking

---

[55] Hastings, R. (2020). How Netflix stayed Relevant Amid the Rapid Changes in the Consumer Video Industry. Harvard Business Review. Retrieved from https://hbr.org

opportunities, enabling you to exchange ideas, share best practices, and build professional connections.

2. Online Courses and Webinars. If getting away is not practical or in your budget, taking online courses and webinars provides flexibility and accessibility, allowing you to learn at your own pace and convenience. With a wide range of topics and formats available, you can choose courses that align with your interests, goals, and schedule. Online learning platforms offer interactive modules, video lectures, quizzes, and assignments, enabling you to acquire new skills and knowledge in a structured and engaging manner. I have learned a great deal from webinars in recent months as I sought for help in how to go about writing and publishing this book.

3. Reading and Research. Reading relevant literature, scholarly articles, and industry reports is a time-honored method of continuing education. By staying abreast of the latest research, trends, and advancements in your field, you expand your knowledge and resource base, deepen your understanding, and gain valuable insights that inform your work. Whether you prefer books, journals, or blogs, regular reading exposes you to diverse perspectives and ideas, fueling your intellectual curiosity and creativity. Do not simply read for information. Look for principles that you can adapt and apply to your own work.

4. Networking and Mentoring. Engaging with peers, mentors, and industry professionals is a powerful way to learn and grow. I have to admit that i am not a fan of networking events nut I have to make an effort if I want to stay relative, visible and innovative, Networking events, professional associations, and mentorship programs provide

opportunities to exchange ideas, seek advice, and learn from others' experiences. By connecting with those who share your interests and aspirations, you expand your professional network, gain valuable insights, and access new opportunities for collaboration and learning.

5. Round Table Discussions. This is my favorite way to learn and grow. In the right setting and with the right people, great ideas are bounced around and built upon and everyone can take away something of value. Round table events promote open and inclusive discussions where every participant can share insights and experiences. This format encourages active participation, leading to a richer exchange of ideas and diverse perspectives. Attendees can engage in real-time problem-solving and brainstorming, often leading to innovative solutions and new strategies.

One of the benefits of round table events is the promotion of organic networking and relationship-building among peers, industry experts, and thought leaders. These connections can be invaluable for future collaboration and knowledge sharing. The interactive nature of these events ensures that learning is dynamic and engaging, as opposed to passive learning methods like lectures or presentations.

Discussions can be tailored to specific topics or challenges, making the learning highly focused and applicable. This targeted approach ensures that participants gain actionable insights and practical knowledge that can be immediately implemented in their work or studies.

Enrichment

Continuing education offers a multitude of benefits that enrich your personal and professional life.

1. Skill Development. Continuously updating your skills and knowledge enhances your capabilities and expertise, making you more effective and proficient in your work. Whether you are mastering recent technologies, honing your communication skills, or learning strategic planning techniques, ongoing education equips you with the newest and most effective tools needed to excel in your field. In the process of writing this book, I watched a few training videos on how to better use Microsoft Word. They turned out to be very valuable and saved me a lot of time.

2. Career Advancement. Investing in continuous learning can open doors to new career opportunities, advancement, and growth. Employers value employees who demonstrate a commitment to professional growth, recognizing the contributions of individuals who are proactive, adaptable, and innovative. By acquiring new skills and staying current with industry trends, you position yourself for success and increase your marketability in the workplace.

3. Adaptability. In today's rapidly changing world, adaptability is a critical skill for navigating uncertainty and seizing opportunities. By staying informed and flexible, you can adapt to shifting circumstances, embrace change, and thrive in dynamic environments. I experience the need for this often as I am called on to speak in different countries and cultural settings. Continuous learning equips you with the knowledge, resources, and confidence needed to overcome challenges and emerge stronger than before. Remember, a fossil is a creature that missed the opportunity to transition.

4. Personal Growth and Fulfillment. Beyond professional benefits, continuing education enriches your personal life, bringing growth, discovery, and awareness. Learning new

skills, exploring new interests, and pursuing lifelong passions opens the doors to a variety of options for self-expression, creativity, and personal fulfillment. Whether you're mastering a musical instrument, studying a foreign language, or seeking to grow spiritually, lifelong learning nourishes your mind, body, and spirit, enriching your life in profound and meaningful ways.

Conclusion

Continuing education is a cornerstone of personal and professional growth. It enables you to stay relevant, adaptable, and competitive in a rapidly changing world. By committing to ongoing education, you invest in yourself, your career, and your future, unlocking new opportunities, expanding your horizons, and realizing your full potential. No matter the method you apply, the pursuit of knowledge is a journey that enriches your mind, broadens your perspective, and enhances the quality of your work product. Embrace the power of continuous learning, and let your curiosity be your guide on the path to success and fulfillment as you maximize your sweet spot.

Personal Challenge

1. Set up a reading list of books, internet articles, journals, and magazines that are relevant to your area of learning. Watching YouTube videos is good to a point, but there is something about reading that makes your brain process information in a way that makes it stick.[56]

2. Search out and set aside time to attend a conference, webinar, or professional group meeting outside of your industry.

3. Micro certification. Take a course in one small area that will help in your personal or professional life. It could take an hour, a day, or a week. Learn something new ,expand your knowledge in your field, and get a piece of paper that says you did it.

---

[56] Sweatt, Lydia. "Why Reading Books is Better than Watching Television." Success, Success Magazine, 23 Oct. 2017

"Evaluation is the systematic determination of a subjects, merit, worth and significance, using criteria governed by a set of standards."

Michael Scrivener
Author and Philosopher

CHAPTER 22
Evaluate

Assessing Performance

Have you ever listened to a recording or watched a video of yourself delivering a speech or presentation. If you are just starting out, it is the most painful exercise. Yet, as a young minister, I made it a point to do just that. As a teenager, I was told I would never make a public speaker. It was meant as a simple instruction as I considered a career, not to be critical or destructive. So when I chose to answer the calling to be a minister, it was with a little trepidation, a good helping of grit, not to mention a lot of help from above, that I committed to a journey of learning and self evaluation.

In those days the recordings were a simple process made directly to cassette. Early in the the week I would put my headphones and listen. No need to take notes. Every stutter, hesitation and every other mistake was indelibly imprinted on my brain. Each week I promised myself to never go through that pain again but each week I would go back for more. At first, I would make a conscious effort to be better and after a while, "muscle memory" kicked in and my speaking style became more natural as I incorporated humor, pathos, conviction and compassion into my messages. I still listen to a recording now and then to keep me on my toes.

Evaluation is essential for improvement in any endeavor. It serves as a means of assessing performance and identifying strengths and weaknesses. Whether by actively seeking feedback from others, or a systematic self-evaluation, you gain valuable perspectives and insights that could be of immense importance. Evaluation is important in fine-tuning what is already working and identifying the areas that are not. It helps breed an attitude of excellence where all involved are empowered to strive for greater things and achieve their full potential.

Contribute to Your Own Success

Seeking feedback from mentors, peers, and team leaders offers several benefits that enhance the quality of your work and contribute to your overall success.

1. Identifying Blind Spots. Evaluation and feedback are crucial in identifying blind spots in both life and work. They provide an external perspective, revealing areas you may overlook due to biases or routines. This is something I have gone through even with the writing f this book. Because I have been working g on it for so long, I know what I want to say and believe I said it clearly. That is until my editor got a look at my work and took me to task to rewrite or clarify many points. Constructive feedback [57] highlights strengths and weaknesses, offering insights into behaviors or practices that need improvement. Regular evaluations encourage self-awareness and adaptive processes. By actively seeking and embracing feedback, you can address shortcomings and make informed decisions about areas you cannot readily see for yourself. Once you've identified your blind spots, the next step is to think about how these insights can fuel your learning and personal growth.

2. Learning and Growth. An honest assessment offers opportunities for learning and growth, enabling you to expand your knowledge, learn new skills, and refine your approach. It offers key insights into your performance, highlighting areas for improvement and reinforcing

---

[57] Notice I did not say "constructive criticism". Anyone can find fault. What you want is someone who can show you WHY you went wrong and HOW to fix it.

strengths. When you learn to see feedback as a learning opportunity rather than a judgment, you can turn mistakes and failures into fuel for improvement and progress. Defend your work when you have to and grow when you need to with the feedback you receive from others. This not only makes you a better person, it could serve to develop some important relationships.

3. Building Relationships. Seeking feedback opens new areas of communication and collaboration, strengthening relationships with mentors, peers, and disciples. Take the opportunity to learn humility, receptivity while creating an environment of trust and mutual respect. These interactions provide feedback so people can address misunderstandings and adjust behaviors to strengthen connections. When done right, this process produces transparency, which is essential for nurturing healthy, productive relationships. This, in turn leads to better productivity.

4. Enhancing Performance. By incorporating feedback into your work, you can enhance the quality of your output and achieve higher levels of performance. Whether itis refining a presentation, revising a report, or adjusting your approach to a project, feedback provides actionable insights that drive improvement and excellence. With the right attitude, feedback and evaluation should contribute to a supportive environment where you feel valued and understood, enhancing individual and team function.

Incorporating Feedback

Effectively incorporating feedback into your work requires a thoughtful and proactive approach. It's one thing to listen to some feedback but it only does you any good if you are willing to act on it. Here are some strategies to consider.

1. Be Open-minded. Approach feedback with an open mind and a willingness to listen. Be receptive to different perspectives and viewpoints, even if they challenge your own. Remember that feedback is not a reflection of your worth or abilities; it is an opportunity for growth and improvement. If you go in thinking you know everything, you will never learn anything.

2. Ask for Specific Feedback. When seeking feedback, be specific about what you need. Ask questions that prompt actionable and insightful analysis, such as "What are the strengths of this project?" and "What are the most critical areas you think could be improved?" When your specifics are addressed, you may ask for further input based on their expertise and knowledge.

3. Consider the Source. Consider the source of the feedback and their knowledge of the subject matter. Feedback from mentors, peers, and supervisors may vary in depth and relevance, so weigh each perspective accordingly. To use a little hyperbole to illustrate this, you would not consult a plumber if you had a problem with blocked arteries. While the principle of clearing blocked pipes may illustrate the general situation, you need the expertise of a heart specialist to evaluate and treat the issue.

4. Reflect and Sum Up. Take time to reflect on the feedback you receive and consider how it can be applied to your situation. Identify actionable steps for improvement and incorporate them into your workflow. Occasionally, this could result in having to dismantle the entire process and go

back to the beginning, but do not be too quick to make drastic changes. Remember, the point of seeking feedback is to refine and enhance what you are doing and how you work in your sweet spot.

5. Express Gratitude. Express appreciation to those who provide feedback. Acknowledge the time and effort they have invested in helping you grow and improve, and let them know that their feedback is valued and appreciated. Obviously, when engaging professional feedback, gratitude is shown in the fee that you pay. When looking at a peer or team member, look for positive ways to reciprocate. This sets up a willingness to collaborate further in the future to build on the improvements you have achieved.

Conclusion

Evaluation is a vital aspect of personal and professional development, enabling you to assess your performance, identify areas for improvement, and refine your work performance. By embracing feedback as a catalyst for improvement, you can nurture excellence, achieve your goals, and realize your full potential. Remember that feedback is not a reflection of your worth but an opportunity for growth and improvement. Embrace it with humility, openness, and a commitment to steady learning, and watch your life and work grow and flourish as you maximize your sweet spot.

Personal Challenge

Evaluating your life and work can provide deep insights and help you grow. Here are three practical challenges you can undertake.

1.   The 30-Day Reflection Challenge

- Daily Journaling: Commit to writing in a journal every day for 30 days, focusing on key aspects of your life and work. Reflect on your achievements, areas for improvement, and how you spend your time.

- End-of-Challenge Review: At the end of the 30 days, review your entries to identify patterns, recurring themes, or concerns. Use these insights to set new goals or make necessary adjustments in your life.

2.   The Time-Tracking Challenge

- Track Your Time: For one week, meticulously track how you spend each hour of your day. It may help to break it down into 15 or 30-minute segments. Include everything from work tasks and meetings to leisure activities and sleep.

- Analyze and Adjust: At the end of the week, analyze your time log to see where your time is going. Identify areas where you may be spending too much or too little time and make changes to align your time with your priorities.

3.   The "Say No" Challenge

- Set Boundaries: For two weeks, practice saying "no" to non-essential tasks, requests, or activities that do not align with your goals or values. This could be at work or in your personal life.

- Evaluate the Impact: Reflect on how saying "no" affects your productivity, stress levels, and overall satisfaction. This challenge helps you prioritize what truly matters and prevents burnout by avoiding over-commitment.

These challenges encourage self-awareness, discipline, and intentional living, helping you make more informed decisions about your life and work.

"This is the key to time management – to see the value of every moment."

Menachem Mendel Schneerson

Rabbi

CHAPTER 23
The Art of Time Management

While there are many detailed volumes on time management available, these thoughts are presented for your consideration in the context of finding and maximizing your sweet spot.

It has been said that if it were not for the last minute, nothing would ever get done. Maybe I was the one who said that because that is certainly the case for me. Most of my work gets done in the last minute. The art of time management is a skill that can transform the way you approach your work, your personal life, and your overall well-being. By mastering the principles of effective time management, you can maximize productivity, minimize stress, and achieve a greater sense of balance and proficiency.

Time is an elusive currency; its value is often debated, and its expenditure is scrutinized. However, it is never wasted if time spent brings you to a place of understanding and intentionality. The waste is in refusing to understand. A good way to spend an hour is exercising, which boosts energy and improves health. Conversely, scrolling through social media mindlessly for an hour when you need to be doing something important can lead to wasted time and decreased productivity.

In the journey of life, I have encountered countless roads where decisions beckoned me to choose between paths known and unknown. I have come to realize that time spent in contemplation to seek clarity and understanding of various perspectives is never squandered. It is through these processes that I have gained insight and a deeper understanding of the world and my place in it.

Priorities

One of the first steps in effective time management is learning to prioritize tasks based on their importance and urgency. Not all tasks are created equal, and itis essential to distinguish between what is essential and what is merely urgent. To prioritize effectively:

1. Identify Important Tasks. Start by identifying the tasks that are most critical to finding and working in your sweet spot. These are the tasks that will have the most significant impact on your success and should be given top priority. Where possible, consider which tasks may be postponed because they are less important or delegated because they require different expertise.

2. Assess Urgency. Urgency is not always synonymous with importance, so be sure to differentiate between tasks that are time-sensitive and those that are time-consuming. Medical triage is based on this principle. Patients are categorized based on the severity of their conditions, prioritizing treatment for those with life-threatening issues first. It's no good setting a broken bone if the person is bleeding out rapidly. The proper decisions ensure the most critical receive immediate care to maximize survival rates. This approach is sometimes necessary in your life and work.

3. Use Time Management Tools. Utilize time management tools such as to-do lists, calendars, and task management apps to organize and prioritize your tasks effectively. Break larger projects down into smaller, manageable tasks, and assign deadlines to ensure timely completion.

Setting priorities allows you to focus your time and energy on what truly matters and helps secure progress toward your goals and objectives. It minimizes wasted time and effort and, when done properly, ensures that all tasks are completed effectively and in a timely manner.

Setting Deadlines

Deadlines are essential for creating a sense of accountability, motivating you to take action and complete tasks on time. Some people stress out about deadlines and it becomes unproductive. For me, the deadline provides motivation to de done by a certain time and I thrive on the challenge. Jut be sure to have a reasonable finish time in sight. When setting deadlines:

1. Be Realistic. Set deadlines that are both challenging and achievable. Avoid unrealistic expectations that may lead to stress and burnout. Consider factors such as the complexity of the task, available resources, and other commitments when establishing deadlines. Be sure to allow ample time for research, execution, revision, and other unforeseen delays.

2. Break Tasks into Milestones. Break larger projects down into smaller, more manageable milestones, each with its own deadline. Consider the various components of the task and which components may be delegated appropriately. This allows you to make steady progress toward your goals and prevents jobs from becoming overwhelming.

3. Periodic assessment. Regular accountability reports serve as an effective deadline management tool, communicating responsibility and providing motivation. Scheduling check-ins, whether through meetings or progress updates, encourages you to stay focused on your tasks. This structured oversight helps identify potential obstacles early, allowing for timely adjustments.

Setting deadlines helps you maintain focus, manage your time effectively, and ensure that you stay on track toward achieving your goals.

Minimizing Distractions

Distractions can derail your focus and productivity, making it challenging to devote adequate time and attention to producing high-quality work. Here are some ideas to help minimize distractions:

1. Create a Distraction-Free Environment. Designate a dedicated workspace that is free from distractions such as noise, clutter, and interruptions. Eliminate or minimize potential distractions by turning off notifications, closing unnecessary tabs or windows, and setting boundaries with colleagues or family members. If necessary, turn your phone off or leave it in another room.

2. Use Time Blocking. Time blocking involves scheduling specific blocks of time for focused work on particular tasks or projects. During these time blocks, eliminate distractions and devote your full attention to the task at hand. Without realizing it, for years I have used the Pomodoro Technique[58], or something very similar, which involves working in short bursts followed by brief breaks, to maintain focus and productivity.

3. Be in the Moment. Discipline yourself to focus only on the thing at hand. For instance, you could keep a page or file open to jot down random ideas so you can come back to them after you have finished with the task at hand. This way, you will not forget about it, and you won't need to break away

---

[58] Francesco Cirillo, The Pomodoro Technique. ©2006, 2018 Francesco Cirillo

from what you are doing. I have found that this helps me improve my concentration, creativity, and keeps me on track. It is a technique I have found particularly helpful while authoring this book.

Minimizing distractions allows you to work more efficiently, maintain focus, and produce high-quality work that meets or exceeds your expectations. Some people love to have background music while working. As much as I love music, it is a distraction to my writing process. From my time rehearsing with bands to time in the recording studio, I have come to listen to music with appreciation, and a finely tuned assessment, unconsciously trying to figure what a musician was doing and how. So, I have had to make the choice to work in complete silence or I end up working on the music instead of the task at hand. Find out what works best for you in your sweet spot.

Conclusion

The art of time management is a valuable skill that can transform the way you approach your work and your life. By prioritizing tasks, setting deadlines, and minimizing distractions, you can maximize productivity, minimize stress, and get more done. Remember to identify important tasks, assess urgency, and use time management tools to organize and prioritize your work effectively. Set realistic deadlines, break tasks into manageable milestones, and focus on completing high-priority tasks first.

Make sure all these factors work together so you get the most from the time you spend on the various aspects of your life. By mastering the principles of effective time management, you can produce high-quality work while making the most of your time, leading to greater success and satisfaction in all areas of your life.

Personal Challenge

Mastering time management involves strategic planning and disciplined execution.

1. Making lists is a fundamental step; it organizes tasks, prioritizes important activities, and provides a clear roadmap for the day. Whether it's a to-do list or a project checklist, writing things down helps ensure nothing is overlooked.

2. Using an appointment calendar or setting reminders is equally crucial. It helps you keep track of deadlines, meetings, and essential tasks, ensuring that you stay on schedule and manage your commitments effectively.

3. Developing the technique of taking short breaks is another key to maintaining productivity. Regular breaks prevent burnout, improve focus, and refresh the mind, making you more efficient when you return to work.

"Excellence is in the details. Give attention to details and excellence will come."

Perry Paxton

Author

CHAPTER 24
Attention to Detail

If you want to have excellence in your life and work and home in your sweet spot, then attention to detail needs to become an integral part of your process. Whether working on a project, completing a task, or pursuing a goal, paying close attention to the details ensures accuracy, completeness, and quality in your work.

I recall a time in the early days of smart phones when sending a text message became much easier as you would type the actual letter on the onscreen keyboard. Sending and receiving messages became a lot quicker. Having a small keyboard and the thought of typing a message more quickly was exciting and the expectation was that this would speed up communication. That was until people didn't check the spelling before hitting send. I fired off a request to a minister friend to do a small job for me. His reply meant to say, OK, I'll take a shot - except that the "o" on the keyboard is right next to the "i" and he ended up sending a message with a totally different meaning than he intended.

We have laughed about the incident over the years and got some mileage out of the story. The point is that not paying attention to detail could have much more serious implications than a mis-typed word between people who don't use profanity.

Examine, Analyze, Scrutinize

Attention to detail is the practice of thoroughly examining, analyzing, and scrutinizing every aspect of your work to ensure accuracy and precision. It involves being methodical, and diligent in your approach, leaving no detail overlooked. The importance of this discipline can mean the difference between good and great.

1. Accuracy. Attention to detail ensures that your work is free from errors and inconsistencies. By carefully reviewing and verifying information, you can identify and correct mistakes before they impact the quality of your work. Often, these mistakes can end up being costly as a friend and supporter of out refuge in India found out. When she typed out her application for a visa to enter India, she mistyped her first name by interpolating the last two letters. We got all the way from the USA to our first stop in Singapore and went to board the flight to India when they checked her visa and caught the spelling error. They would not let her board till it was fixed and the two little letters typed the wrong way around, ended up costing them the trip and a lot of money. Finding and fixing these errors not only enhances success, but also helps build a reliable reputation and trust with clients and teams.

2. Completeness. Thoroughness in your approach ensures that all necessary components and requirements are addressed and included in your work. By paying attention to the details, you can avoid omissions, oversights, and gaps in your work and enhance its impact and integrity. In the race to place their product on the market, many software programs and apps are plagued with the issue of bug fixes. Not only does this undermine consumer confidence, but it also raises the issue of negative reviews, often tarnishing the reputation of a potentially excellent product.

3. Quality. Attention to detail is a hallmark of excellent work. Over the years I have used tradesmen that have done the job for a reasonable price and they walk away with both of us being satisfied. At other times, I have used Master Craftsmen who go the extra mile with the detail and the quality of their

work and I have very rarely, if ever, had to call on someone at a letter time to repair their work. By demonstrating a commitment to precision, you can produce work that meets or exceeds expectations, reflects professionalism, and earns the admiration and confidence of others. Have you ever booked a hotel based on the online photos, only to find out some features just did not work? Quality is more than what you represent to people – it is what they experience.

Get the Devil Out of the Detail

"The devil is in the detail" as the old saying goes. It is the minute or insignificant elements of a project that can put it over the top or doom it to failure. The devil may lurk there but paying close attention will disarm and remove him.

Attention to detail offers numerous benefits that contribute to your success in various aspects of your life and purpose.

1. Professionalism. Attention to detail is a hallmark of professionalism and competence. By demonstrating a meticulous and thorough approach to your work, you convey reliability, competence, and trustworthiness to others. My son is a professional Graphic Designer and has done a lot of work for me over the years. The cover design of this book is his work. We went back and forth on things like color, layout, font and even the wording and I believe we came up with a very high quality, excellent product.

2. Efficiency. Efficiency is the ability to achieve maximum productivity with minimum wasted effort or expense. It means optimizing resources, time, and energy to accomplish tasks effectively and economically. As we have seen in a previous chapter, Henry Ford broke the mold when it came to implementing a high efficiency production line for his

cars. Though it has been refined over the years it has become the basis for fast, quality work at the manufacturing level. Attention to detail enhances efficiency by minimizing or eliminating errors and revisions.

3. Confidence. When you know that your work is accurate, thorough, and of high quality, you can approach tasks and challenges with confidence, knowing that you have done your due diligence and given your best effort. Your clients can also have confidence that the service or product you are providing for them will perform as promised. If you are a perfectionist like me, getting to the place of confidence in your completed work can be quite a challenge because perfectionists always find something that they can improve on. I found the approach that saved my sanity was learning when I had got to the point where I was the only one who wanted to make adjustments. It took a while but I learned to be confident about my work when it had reached a certain level. It may not have been perfect enough for the perfectionist but when the quality is high anyway, it can be released with confidence.

4. Reputation. Attention to detail builds your reputation and credibility. When others perceive you as someone who pays attention to the details and delivers high-quality work, they are more likely to trust and respect your judgment, recommendations, and contributions.

Rolls-Royce has earned a stellar name through meticulous attention to detail, exemplified in their handcrafted car interiors and precision engines. [59] Each vehicle undergoes rigorous design,

---

[59] Smith, Paul. (2013). Rolls-Royce Motor Cars: The Pursuit of Perfection. Merrell Publishers.

testing, and customization, ensuring superior quality and performance. The company's commitment to detail extends to the smallest elements, like the hand-stitched leather seats and flawless paint finishes. This unwavering focus on craftsmanship and precision has made Rolls-Royce synonymous with luxury, reliability, and engineering brilliance.

Strategies

Paying attention to detail is a skill that can be refined over time. Here are some strategies to help you improve your diligence and maximize your sweet spot.

1. Develop a Systematic Approach. Develop ways to approach your work, consisting of clear processes, procedures, and checklists. Break tasks down into smaller, more manageable steps, some of which you may be able to delegate, and follow a structured workflow to ensure thoroughness and completeness. This not only ensures the quality of your effort, but also enables others to learn and reproduce a strategy that works. I have found the use of checklists, routines and things like templates help streamline the work and minimize mistakes. After all these years of travel, I still use a packing checklist to make sure I don't forget something important.

2. Double-Check Your Work. Take the time to review and double-check your work before finalizing it. Look for errors, inconsistencies, and areas that may need clarification or improvement. Consider enlisting other experts to provide a fresh perspective and identify any overlooked details. Because I work in many cultures around the world, I need to double-check that my writing and teaching work and is understood in a variety of settings. I have had my share of

faux pas because I have said or done something that is totally innocent in one culture but quite offensive in another.

3. Pay Attention to Patterns. Pay attention to patterns, trends, and recurring themes in your work. Some may reinforce your point, while some could prove redundant. Look for commonalities, connections, and discrepancies that may present opportunities for improvement. By analyzing patterns, you can identify areas where attention to detail is particularly important and focus your efforts accordingly.

Those who are old enough to have been around at the time will never forget the Space Shuttle Challenger disaster in 1986. The explosion, just 73 seconds after liftoff, was caused by a failure of O-ring seals in its solid rocket booster. Engineers had noticed potential issues with the O-rings but underestimated their severity, especially in freezing weather conditions. Detailed attention to these warnings and a thorough reassessment of the launch conditions might have prevented the disaster. The tragedy resulted in the loss of seven astronauts' lives and led to significant changes in NASA's safety protocols, emphasizing meticulous detail in engineering and decision-making.[60]

Conclusion

Attention to detail is a critical skill that contributes to accuracy, completeness, and quality in your work product. By paying close attention to the details, you can ensure that your work meets or exceeds expectations, reflects professionalism, and earns the trust and confidence of others. This requires a systematic approach, double-checking your work and looking for patterns. Understand the importance of paying attention to detail and incorporating it into

---

[60] Challenger: A True Story of Heroism and Disaster on the Edge of Space. ©2024 Adam Higginbotham. Simon and Schuster LLC

your work habits. You can enhance your effectiveness, productivity, and success in all aspects of your life.

Personal Challenge

Most of this chapter is a huge personal challenge, so do the following:

1. Address and list the points in this chapter that apply to you and your work.

2. Identify areas in which you need to rework or defend your work.

3. Create checklists before a new project is started, and be prepared to edit them as you go through the job so that the next time you do it, you will have streamlined the process of attention to detail.

"Surround yourself with the best people you can find, delegate authority, and don't interfere."

Ronald Reagan

40th President USA

CHAPTER 25
The Delegation Imperative

Delegation is a crucial skill in the realm of productivity and leadership. It involves entrusting tasks and responsibilities to others, empowering them to contribute to the achievement of common goals. The delegation imperative adds many dimensions to your work and helps free each team member to work in their own sweet spot.

Resource Management

The basis of delegation is effective resource management. Tasks, projects, or responsibilities that can be assigned to others based on their skills and expertise is identified and allocated. Delegation is not about offloading work or avoiding responsibility but rather about leveraging the strengths of team members to achieve collective goals. When this is done correctly, leaders can focus their time and energy on high-priority tasks, while empowering team members to take ownership and contribute to the overall success of the project.

Delegation can also liberate creativity, which may be hiding beneath the surface of team members. Entrusting tasks to capable people frees up time and mental space, inviting fresh perspectives and innovative ideas. Collaborative efforts spark synergy, igniting a creative fire that goes beyond individual limitations. Through delegation, creativity finds wings, soaring to new heights of ingenuity and achievement.

Delegation, when done right, not only enhances productivity but also catalyzes innovation. Take, for example, the story of Google's founders Larry Page and Sergey Brin. With the spectacular growth of the company they had to delegate or face the reality of many points of constraint for their brand. So, in 2014, they delegated much of the company's day-to-day operations to Sundar Pichai, who was then the product chief. By delegating responsibilities, Page and Brin could focus on long-term innovation, while Pichai concentrated on refining Google's core products, such as Chrome and Android. This strategic delegation allowed Google to thrive, improving product quality and expanding its market share. Under Pichai's leadership, Chrome became the world's leading web browser, and Android continued its dominance in the mobile OS market. Delegating responsibilities not only optimized efficiency but also allowed Google's leadership to focus on a broader company vision, ultimately driving more effective outcomes across the organization.[61]

Maximizing Your Team

Not only do I speak at a number of conferences each year, I have organized my fair share. One of the larger conferences involved the coordination of everything from publicity, to venue set up, PA system, vendor booths, Green Room for speakers…the list was pages long. Everyone was assigned an area of responsibility and for the most part, did their jobs well. On the day the conference began, my phone started to ring. For some reason, everyone from the stage and lighting people to the caterers to the parking attendants needed to check in with me. Eventually, I found a trusted assistant, and gave her my phone with instructions to simply assure people that they were doing their job well and they were in place because I trusted them to handle anything that came up. It was a lesson for me.

---

[61] Larry Page and Sergey Brin: Why We're Excited about Alphabet." Google Blog, October 2, 2015.

Delegation is not just about handing out jobs, it is about letting people know that you trust them to get it done.

Delegation offers several benefits for both leaders and team members. Here are some:

1. Increased Productivity. Delegation increases productivity by allowing leaders to distribute tasks to team members based on their strengths and skills. This not only optimizes resource deployment but allows team members to gain ownership and motivation, often leading to more innovative and efficient solutions. Overall, delegation decreases bottlenecks, [62] speeds up project timelines, and leverages diverse skills, leading to enhanced overall productivity and successful project outcomes.

2. Skill Advancement. When leaders delegate tasks, they provide openings for people to expand their skill sets and gain practical experience in areas to which they are best suited. A good manager would not send their best salesperson to learn how to repair production machinery. By appointing others to take charge of specific projects, leaders can facilitate the transfer of knowledge and responsibilities. Over time, this approach not only builds a more capable workforce but also contributes to both personal and organizational growth.

3. Leadership Maturity. Delegation is a cornerstone of effective leadership growth and maturity. Through delegation, leaders can groom successors, empower emerging leaders, growing and expand the organization in all areas, from innovation to

---

[62] For more on this subject see Goldratts development on the Theory of Constraints. Goldratt Eliyahu M. (1984). The Goal: A Process of Ongoing Improvement. North River Press,

final product. Delegation also allows leaders to focus on higher-level strategic initiatives, enabling them to fulfill their role as visionaries and decision-makers.

Challenging Factors

While delegation can be incredibly powerful, it's not without its pitfalls. Let's now explore some of the common challenges leaders face when delegating and how to overcome them. None of these are insurmountable, but being aware of them will help streamline the solution.

1. Lack of Trust. Delegating tasks requires a level of trust between leaders and team members. Leaders must have confidence in the abilities of their team members to execute tasks effectively and responsibly. If that is not communicated and demonstrated, you might as well do the job yourself. Conversely, team members must trust that their leaders will provide support, guidance, and resources as needed.

2. Unclear Communication. Effective delegation relies on clear and open communication. Communicate expectations, guidelines, and deadlines clearly to ensure that everyone understands their roles and responsibilities. With most major undertakings in my experience, I have come to know the value of writing down expectations - whether through a formal job description of a simple email or text message. Ongoing communication is necessary for monitoring progress, providing feedback, and addressing any issues that may arise.

3. Risk of Micromanagement. One common pitfall of delegation is the temptation to micromanage. Leaders may feel the need to closely monitor the progress of delegated

tasks, leading to unnecessary interference and undermining the autonomy of team members. Itis essential to strike a balance between requiring accountability and allowing individuals the freedom to take ownership of their work.

4. Gaps in Skill and Knowledge. Delegating tasks requires careful consideration of team members' skills, expertise, and capacity. Leaders must assess whether they have the necessary abilities and knowledge to complete delegated tasks successfully. In cases where skill or knowledge gaps exist, leaders may need to provide training, support, or access to resources to ensure successful task execution, thus enhancing the team's sweet spot. Have you ever been at this point? It feels like it would be simpler to do the job yourself instead of taking the time to teach someone else. That may be true if its a 'one-off' situation. But if you need to repeat something , take the time to train others. There will come a point when you will be happy you did.

Conclusion

Delegation is a critical skill for effective leadership and teamwork. By entrusting tasks and responsibilities to others, leaders can maximize productivity, growth, and enhance collaboration within teams. Although delegation may pose some challenges, these can be overcome through clear communication, support, and strategic planning. By employing strategies for a successful delegation process, leaders can leverage the strengths of their team members to achieve common goals and drive organizational success. Effective delegation is a win-win for leaders and team members alike, enabling both to thrive in their sweet spot and contribute to the overall success of the organization.

Personal Challenge

1. Develop a table or flow chart of your process from start to finish, connecting each step with the skills and /or personnel to accomplish it. Keep in mind that outsourcing some parts of the process would be more efficient than doing it in-house.

2. Come up with a metric to rate the efficiency of each part of the process. This could be done by engaging consultants that specialize in this field or by using available staff to do this on an ongoing basis.

3. Write job descriptions for each role, defining responsibilities and authority, chain of leadership, etc. This can and should be rewritten as you grow and develop so you can maximize your sweet spot.

"The important thing is to not stop asking questions. Curiosity has its own reason for existing."

Albert Einstein

Physicist

233

CHAPTER 26
Six Honest Serving Men

I keep six honest serving men
(They taught me all I knew).
Their names are What and Why and When
And How and Where and Who.
I send them over land and sea,
I send them east and west.
But after they have worked for me,
I give them all a rest.

Rudyard Kipling's poem[63] introduces the idea of the "six honest serving men"—what, why, when, how, where, and who. These questions invite readers to reflect on the power of inquiry in shaping understanding and perception, guiding us in various endeavors, including the search for one's "sweet spot." The sweet spot, in this context, refers to the intersection of passion, skill, job, and opportunity, where a person can thrive personally and professionally.

In my own life, the moment I began asking these questions was when I realized that my passions weren't just hobbies, but a guide to finding my purpose. Finding your sweet spot is a journey marked by exploration and reflection. It requires a willingness to engage deeply with your interests and values and a commitment to taking actionable steps toward fulfillment. Embracing this journey with the help of Kipling's "Six Honest Serving Men" can lead to profound insights and a more satisfying and successful life.

---

[63] https://www.kiplingsociety.co.uk/poem/poems_serving.htm

Understanding the Six Honest Serving Men

Kipling's six honest serving men are foundational for critical thinking and problem-solving. Each question serves a unique purpose in illuminating various aspects of our experiences. Have you ever wondered why you're drawn to certain activities but not others?

1. Why? Later in the poem, Kipling singles this out as the most important question by far because it delves into motivation. Why do you pursue certain activities or careers? Understanding your primary motivations can reveal whether your pursuits align with your values and aspirations. When you define a resonating "why," you are more likely to be living your purpose.

2. What? This question encourages us to identify and define our passions, skills, and interests. It is essential to articulate what you genuinely enjoy and excel at. For instance, what activities bring you joy? What subjects captivate you? Understanding the "what" is the first step in discovering your sweet spot.

3. When? I have missed my fair share of opportunities. Looking back, I believe that I missed the importance of asking when. Timing plays a critical role in finding your sweet spot. The "when" involves recognizing the right moments to seize opportunities or engage in specific activities. It may relate to personal circumstances, market conditions, or phases in life that align with your goals.

4. How? You may have figured out the answers to all the other five questions, but without the correct methods and strategies, you are not achieving anything. How do you improve your skills? How do you market yourself or your

products? Understanding the "how" allows you to build a pathway toward your sweet spot, transforming dreams into actionable steps.This is probably the question I am asked most when I am helping leaders find their way. Once they have figured out the "why" they want to know how.

5. Where? Having lived in a few places, this has always been an important question for me. Each place I have lived, studied and worked has had a profound influence on where I am today, what I do and how I do it. The "where" refers to the environment and context in which you operate. Some people thrive in collaborative settings, while others prefer solitude. Identifying where you are most productive and inspired can help you align your purpose with appropriate environments. "Where" is not always a practical location. Sometimes it can be a more philosophical space in which your worldview is formed or refined and you grow.

6. Who? Finally, the "who" encompasses relationships and networks. Who are the people that influence and support you? Building a network of mentors, peers, and disciples can open doors and provide guidance on your journey toward finding your sweet spot.

For me, the answers to these questions have not turned out to be a one time discovery. As I grow in my work, another part of the picture is revealed. I often think that even when I get to a point where I have to physically slow down, I will still discover another part of the answer and have something to achieve till they may literally have to carry me out on my shield.

Applying the Six Honest Serving Men

Finding your sweet spot involves a comprehensive exploration of these six questions. Here is how you can apply them in a structured way:

1. Investigate Motivations. Dig deeper into the "why." Ask yourself why these interests are important. Are they tied to your values? Understanding your motivations can guide your decision-making and help ensure that your pursuits are meaningful.

2. Introspection. This harkens back to the need for evaluation. Start with the "what." List your interests and passions. Consider taking assessments or engaging in exercises that reveal your strengths and weaknesses. This process can clarify what truly matters to you.

3. Assess Timing. Consider the "when." Reflect on your current life situation. Are you in a place where you can invest time and energy into pursuing your sweet spot? Timing can influence the viability of pursuing certain paths, so be mindful of external circumstances.

4. Plan Your Approach. Address the "how." Create an initial plan that outlines three to five actionable steps to improve your skills or transition into new opportunities. This could involve education, networking, or practical experience. Establish a timeline and benchmarks to measure progress.

5. Find Your Environment. Evaluate the "where." An idyllic beach on a tropical island may not be the best place to sell wool sweaters, but it could be a great spot to rent beach chairs, umbrellas and sell cold drinks. Identify settings that inspire you and enhance your productivity. This could involve choosing a workplace that aligns with your working

style or creating a home environment conducive to creativity and focus.

6. Build Your Network. Finally, examine the "who." Develop relationships with people who can support you in your journey. This might include mentors, peers in your field, or even communities of like-minded individuals. Networking can lead to new opportunities and insights.

Challenges on the Journey

Kipling's words remind us that every question leads to a deeper understanding, and in our journey toward finding fulfillment, these questions serve as guideposts. While the six honest serving men provide a framework for exploration, the journey to finding your sweet spot is not without challenges. Self-doubt, fear of failure, and external pressures can obscure our vision. We have already looked at navigating these obstacles in previous chapters. Seeking feedback, remaining open to change, and allowing for reiterations in our approach can help us stay aligned with our goals.

It is important to remember that the concept of the sweet spot is not static; it can evolve over time. Life changes, career shifts, and personal growth can all influence our interests and capabilities. Thus, applying the six questions periodically throughout life can ensure that we remain aligned with our current aspirations and circumstances.

Remember, reevaluating is much different from second-guessing. Reevaluation helps look for ways of improving and growing. Second guessing introduces doubt and is often based on fear.

Socrates, the classical Greek philosopher, epitomized the importance of asking the right questions to find purpose. Through his method of inquiry, known as the Socratic Method [64], he encouraged others to question their beliefs and assumptions. By asking probing questions like "What is justice?" and "What is the good life?" Socrates challenged Athenians to think deeply about their values and the purpose of their actions. His relentless questioning led his followers to seek wisdom and self-awareness, helping them to discover their own purposes. Socrates' legacy illustrates how critical questioning can lead to profound personal and philosophical enlightenment.

Conclusion

While some may be more driven than others to question what they see and experience, we all have an innate drive to know things. Each question represents a thread in the tapestry of life, weaving together a complex montage of exploration and discovery.

Rudyard Kipling's six honest serving men offer valuable tools for navigating the intricate process of discovery. By systematically asking why, what, when, how, where, and who, you can gain clarity and direction in your personal and professional endeavors. This reflective practice enhances your ability to adapt and thrive in a dynamic world and will aid in bringing clarity and focus. Using these "six honest serving men" will not only help you realize and define your sweet spot, but it will also help you refine and maximize it.

---

[64] https://www.britannica.com/topic/Socratic-method

Personal Challenge

These questions have helped shape countless lives, but how can we apply them daily to foster real growth? Let's explore...

1. **Ask Reflective Questions**

   Example: What did I learn from today's experiences?

   Purpose: Reflective questions encourage self-awareness and help you evaluate your actions, thoughts, and decisions. By regularly reflecting, you can identify patterns in your behavior and make more informed choices moving forward.

2. **Ask Solution-Oriented Questions**

   Example: What can I do differently to overcome this challenge?

   Purpose: These questions shift your focus from problems to solutions. Instead of dwelling on what went wrong, you direct your energy toward finding constructive ways to improve or resolve the situation. This approach fosters a proactive mindset and encourages problem-solving.

3. **Ask Forward-Looking Questions**

   Example: What steps can I take today to achieve my long-term goals?

   Purpose: Forward-looking questions help you plan and align your daily actions with your long-term aspirations. By consistently asking these types of questions, you stay motivated and focused on your goals, making it easier to track progress and make necessary adjustments.

By incorporating these types of questions into your daily routine, you can foster personal growth, find solutions to challenges, and maintain a clear vision of your future.

WHY	...must we do this?	...does it matter?	...why is there a need right now?
WHAT	...makes this important?	...makes this positive/negative ?	...is hindering the progress?
WHERE	...can we make this work?	...do we find out how to improve?	...will this take us further on?
WHEN	...can we expect results?	...is it acceptable/Unacceptable?	...should we ask for help?
HOW	...is this one different?	...does this apply to our future?	...do we maintain this?
WHO	...who is responsible?	...are the key personnel?	...sets the pace?

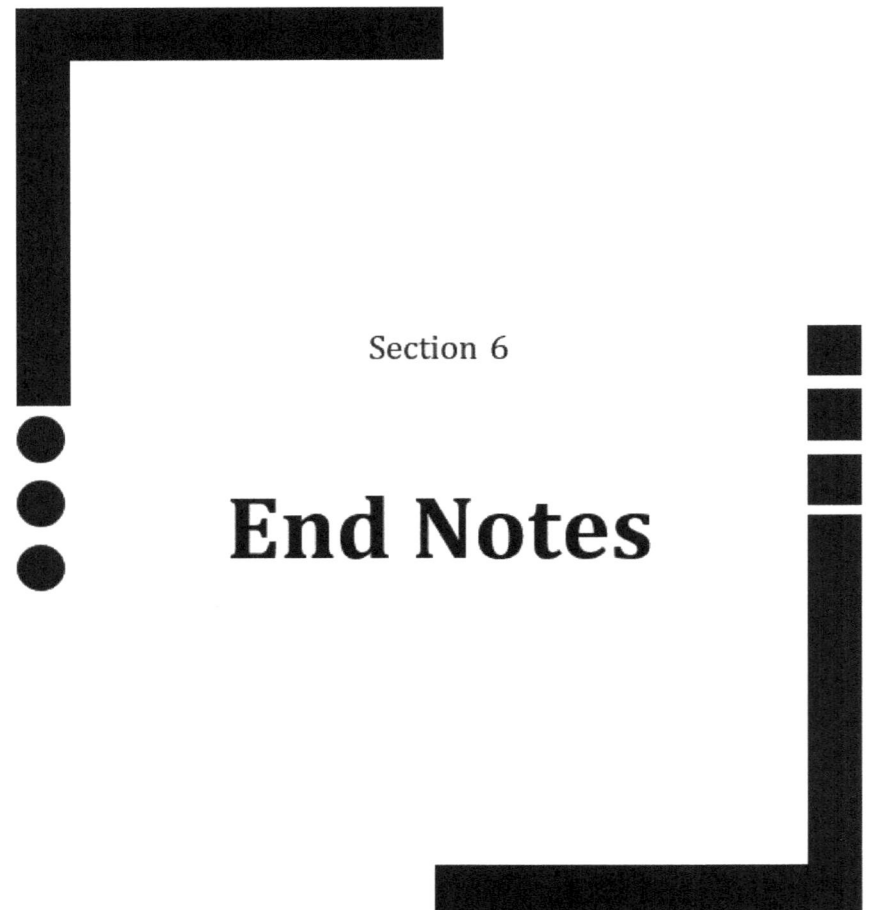

Section 6

End Notes

"Habit formation is the process by which a behavior becomes progressively more automatic through repetition. The more you repeat an activity, the more the structure of your brain changes to become efficient at that activity."

James Clear

Author- Atomic Habits

CHAPTER 27
Practice Your Sweet Spot

My grandmother bought me a cheap guitar for my 13th birthday because I wanted to learn to play. I did not take formal lessons at that time, but I bought myself a book and spent hours practicing every day. I knew a little about music theory from my piano lessons, so I had some idea of what I wanted to achieve. I would practice the shape of the chords, changing the chords and coordinating it all with my strumming. Eventually, I got to the point where I was able to play in public without embarrassing myself... too much. My only regret is that I did not continue to develop my skills on the guitar. I went on to other things in my life and worked at growing my skills in those areas.

In the adventure that has been my life so far, I have learned a few lessons about simply knowing how to do something to become proficient at it and then how to become excellent at it. Here are some of the things I have learned.

When you are on a good thing, stick to it

As a teenager in the 1970s, I saw an ad on TV for Mortien, a brand of insect spray in Australia. They had several very catchy commercials that ran through the decades. From the 1930s till 1986, the tagline was. "When you're on a good thing, stick to it". It became a cultural Aussie catchphrase and was applied to many areas of life - education, sports, careers, and even relationships.

Success often stems from consistent effort in a particular area of strength or passion. When you identify a sweet spot that brings a positive impact to your life, find ways to stay with it. Leverage your talents and hone them further. By continuously engaging in activities where you excel, you reinforce your skills and build a solid foundation for long-term growth. Recognize what works and double down on it rather than constantly switching paths. Staying the course allows for deeper expertise and can lead to greater rewards over time. This doesn't mean avoiding innovation or adaptation but rather focusing on areas where you can make the most impact.

Build Muscle Memory

Muscle memory refers to the process by which repeated practice of a physical task engrains it into your memory, making it second nature. This concept is not limited to physical activities but applies to any skill, including intellectual and creative pursuits. Through consistent practice, actions become more automatic and efficient, reducing the cognitive load required to perform them. This frees up mental resources for more complex problem-solving or creativity. In his book, Atomic Habits, author James Clear makes the point that it is the frequency of repetition that builds this type of muscle memory.[65]

In the context of practicing your sweet spot, building muscle memory means dedicating time to repetitive, focused practice in your area of strength. This consistent practice leads to proficiency and can significantly enhance performance, allowing you to perform tasks with precision and confidence.

Reflect and Adapt

In my office, I have a comfortable recliner that is purposely pointed away from my desk and my computer screen. I often refer to it as my 'think' chair. If I run into a block in my workflow, or am processing a new idea, I sit back in that chair, close my eyes, and simply spend the time thinking through the issue. Some of my

---

[65] Atomic Habits. Chapter 11. ©2018 James Clear. Penguin Random House LLC

greatest ideas and successes in life have come to me as I have sat and simply reflected on what I want to achieve.

Reflection and adaptation are crucial for continuous improvement and sustained success. Regular reflection involves assessing your performance, understanding what worked, what did not, and identifying areas for improvement. This introspective process helps you learn from your experiences and refine your strategies.

Adaptation, on the other hand, is about making necessary adjustments based on this reflection. It means being flexible and responsive to changing circumstances and the latest information. In the context of practicing your sweet spot, it ensures that you don't become stagnant or complacent. By reflecting on your progress and adapting your approach, you can maintain momentum and continue growing in your chosen field.

Be Patient

If you have got to this point in the book, you have read the chapter on the Journey to Overnight Success. Life is much more than a two-hour movie, a one-hour drama, or a half-hour sitcom, where problems or issues are identified, a solution is worked out, and by the end, everyone lives happily ever after. Unless, of course, they are planning a sequel and want to end on a cliffhanger. My point is that life is a series of episodes and sequels that require a lot of patience and application to see you through to a successful conclusion. Not every episode of your life will have a positive conclusion or happy ending. Build on previous experiences, taking time to learn the lessons.

Patience is a vital component of mastering any skill or area of expertise. Achieving excellence often requires sustained effort over an extended period. Instant success is rare, and setbacks are part of the journey. Patience helps you stay committed during challenging times and maintain your motivation despite slow progress.

It is important to recognize that skill advancement is a gradual process, and significant achievements often result from years of dedication and hard work. In living your purpose, patience allows you to persevere, steadily build your capabilities, and achieve an elevated level of mastery. This long-term perspective can help you stay focused and stay in your sweet spot.

Stay in Your Lane

One of my pet peeves in life is getting stuck behind a vehicle that is traveling too slowly in the wrong lane on a highway. As you identify your sweet spot in the journey of life, it is important to know where you are headed, which route to take to get there, and the pace at which you need to travel to get there in a meaningful way and time. Of course, there will be times when you come upon the slowpokes or some other hazards and must change lanes to go around them. But that should be more of a periodic adjustment so that you can continue without further hindrance.

"Staying in your lane" means focusing on your strengths and not getting distracted by what others are doing. It's about recognizing your unique abilities and concentrating your efforts where you can excel. This principle encourages you to avoid comparing yourself to others and instead, commit to your path.

By staying in your lane, you can allocate your time and energy to areas where you have the greatest potential for success. It maintains a sense of purpose and direction, allowing you to develop your skills deeply and effectively. In the broader context, this focus helps you make significant contributions in your area of expertise and stand out as a specialist.

Conclusion

Living your purpose is not a one-and-done event. Once you have figured out what you are meant to do – the things that line up with your skills and passion - you need to make sure that you put the right mechanics in place to keep you in your sweet spot. There are too many distractions in life that would steal your attention and distract you from your ultimate purpose. Be vigilant to avoid camping at a destination along the road to your destiny. Discover your sweet spot and LIVE YOUR PURPOSE.

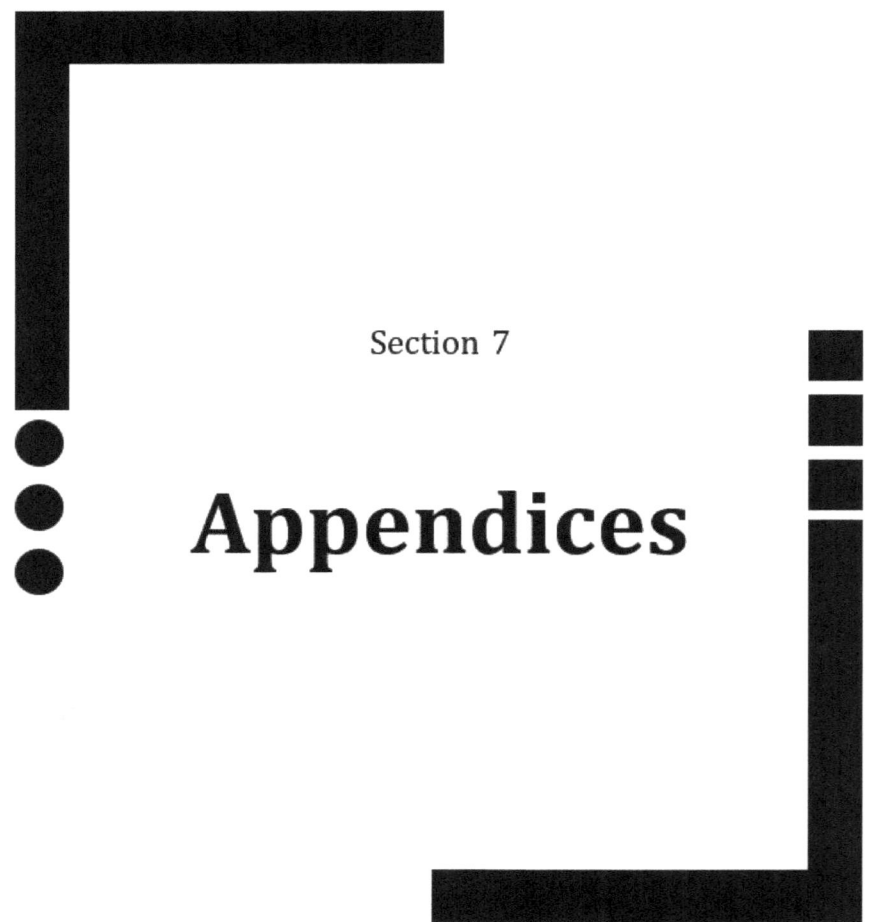

Section 7

Appendices

Appendix 1
Contrasting Being Burned Out and Fired Up

The reason many people suffer burnout is not because they are doing too much, but that they are doing too much of the wrong thing. The following contrasts are to help you understand which camp you are in; those who are "burned out" (or on your way to being so) or those who are "fired up". I am not saying that the comparison is always to be viewed in extreme terms. There is a spectrum – the scale goes from "slight" to "extreme". The list is not exhaustive but is meant to initiate an approach to help you recognize where you are as you embark on the journey to find your sweet spot.

1. "Burned out" perceives the entire world as against them.
   "Fired up" finds their place in the world.

2. "Burned out" sees obstacles.
   "Fired up" looks for opportunity.

3. "Burned out" sees failure as the end.
   "Fired up" rises from the ashes.

4. "Burned out" blames others for lack of success.
   "Fired up" takes what they already have and uses it to find success.

5. "Burned out" is never satisfied, yet will not pursue something more.
   "Fired up" takes what they already have and builds upon that.

6. "Burned out" looks for ways to get a handout.
   "Fired up" looks for ways to give a hand up.

7. "Burned out" spreads negativity based on the past.
   "Fired up" spreads positivity based on hope for the future.

8. "Burned out" has relationships based on fulfilling their needs. "Fired up" has relationships on many levels.

9. "Burned out" is only focused on their rights. "Fired up" is focused on their responsibilities.

10. "Burned out" is critical and judgmental. "Fired up" is passionate and empowering.

11. "Burned out" plays on the emotions of others. "Fired up" releases the passion of others.

12. "Burned out" is afraid that things will get worse. "Fired up" has faith that things will get better.

Appendix 2
Transformational Introspection

1. **Do I have a sense of purpose/destiny in my life?**

   Activity is not equal to productivity. Don't spend too much time on trivial or unimportant things.

2. **Am I building at the expense of the people around me?**

   Often, we need to remind ourselves that without the people around us, it would be difficult – if not impossible – to grow. In your journey, remember to bring others with you.

3. **Is my skill level keeping pace with the progress I am making?**

   Increasing skills and success often result in increasing influence. We need to be sure we are equipped to manage these dynamics in every way.

4. **Who are my key relationships, and how can I properly invest in them?**

   While finding our sweet spot may identify relationships that are a distraction, it is imperative to identify those that are important. Keep family at the top of the list of "key relationships" to nurture.

5. **Do I have an accurate picture of the current situation in which I find myself?**

   Seasons change as life goes on. You do not plant seeds during a drought, nor do you sit back during times of harvest. Identify and recognize your times and seasons.

6. **Are there lifestyle habits or patterns that I need to moderate to live and work in my sweet spot?**

The things we focus on enhance or distract from our purpose. If you need to spend increased time on a hobby to distract you from work stress, maybe it is time to investigate how you can improve your work situation.

7. **Is my physical, emotional, and spiritual life in harmony?**

Neglect or over-emphasis in any of these areas at the expense of others will keep your life off balance. Seek help if you need to.

8. **Am I wasting time on anything?**

We all have only 24 hours in a day. It is hard to "switch off" when you are a driven person, but discipline yourself to take a break when you need to and do not neglect the other important things in your life.

9. **How can I educate myself to become a better person?**

Surround yourself with the right people – people you trust with your life. Build relationships with people that will lift you up. Growing in life is not just about taking more classes.

Appendix 3
Evaluating Your Focus

We can all find ourselves becoming stale or complacent as time goes by. It is essential to take time to regularly reevaluate yourself - what you do and how you do it. As your skill set grows, you may need to make adjustments to stay in your sweet spot. Technology has changed exponentially in recent times and will continue to do so in the future. For example, what took hours of manual research can now be accomplished in a few seconds, using AI.

Here are some steps you can take to evaluate your focus.

1. **Identify a single area in your life that is the most important at the time**

    This may vary with the differing seasons, in which you find yourself. You may want to differentiate between career, family, social, and spiritual. Get input from mentors and peers, where necessary.

2. **Can you honestly say you are on track to fulfill your mission**

    Sometimes, unexpected circumstances may bump you off track. Health issues, family dynamics, natural disasters, and many other factors can all play a part in how you travel a chosen path. (Who expected what the Covid pandemic would do to our world)? Even when things are going well, consider if there may be an opportunity to improve or expand.

3. Inventory your available resources

This means taking a critical look at the skills you have personally, or those that are readily available to you - staff or partners. The loftiest plans are worthless without the means to achieve them.

4. Establish the scope of your influence

What/who/where is your target demographic? Whether you are selling fridge magnets, or luxury jets, the right people need to see you. Understanding these factors will help you to recognize and prioritize your time and resources.

5. Be willing to pass up on an opportunity to attain your highest goal

It is important to remember that good is the enemy of the best. Learn to tell the difference between stepping stones and obstacles.

6. Surround yourself with the right mix of people

You will need a cheer squad, a maintenance crew, and someone who will challenge you when needed. Having people who say yes to everything really does not help you to achieve anything.

7. Designate leisure time

For some, this means hurrying up and having fun. That may be necessary on occasion, but you need to do something other than your work stuff. If you don't have the time for this, go back to the start ,evaluate all the things you do, and figure out which things you can designate or eliminate.

Appendix 4
People Who Will not be Helped

I have been involved in various leadership roles since the 1980's, and I have had the desire to help everyone. But I have learned through sometimes better experiences that I cannot help a person who is not willing to meet me at least halfway.

Here is a list of the major characteristics of people I have not been able to help – some not at all and some only part way.

Evading Responsibility

People who evade responsibility often shirk their duties, blaming others for their failures. They avoid accountability, making excuses to sidestep obligations. This undermines trust and team dynamics, leading to frustration and inefficiency. Such individuals prioritize self-interest over collective goals, harming both personal and organizational growth.

Dodging Accountability

The artful dodger hampers progress and fosters a toxic environment. By not owning up to their actions, they prioritize self-preservation over integrity for themselves and those who work with them, negatively impacting everyone involved. Often, they will bounce from one job or organization to another, and this behavior is reflected in their personal life.

Pessimistic Perspective

People with a pessimistic perspective often expect the worst, focusing on negative outcomes. They tend to overlook positives, dwelling on potential failures and obstacles. This outlook often leads to decreased motivation and morale, influencing others with their negativity. Their constant skepticism can result in an unteachable attitude and, thereby an unproductive life.

Unimaginative Vision

People with an unimaginative vision often stick to conventional thinking, resisting innovation and creativity. They prefer familiar paths, avoiding risks and new ideas. This mindset limits potential and stifles growth, leading to stagnant environments. Their reluctance to embrace change can impede progress and diminish opportunities for advancement and success.

Delusional Life

This person lives detached from reality, holding false beliefs despite contrary evidence. They often create fantasies to escape the truth, ignoring practical concerns. The resulting disconnect can lead to poor decision-making and strained relationships, as their distorted perceptions clash with the real world, ultimately leading to disappointment and conflict.

Reluctant to invest the effort

Avoiding challenges and seeking shortcuts are the primary markers of this type of person. They lack commitment and perseverance, preferring comfort over hard work. This attitude negates their value as a team member and limits their opportunities to realize goals. Because of this they often experience a stagnant life and career.

Pretentiousness

People who are pretentious project false airs of importance or sophistication. They often exaggerate their abilities, knowledge, or status to impress others. This can come across as insincere and off-putting, creating barriers in genuine relationships. Their need for admiration and validation often masks insecurity and a lack of authenticity.

Disingenuous

People who are disingenuous often conceal their true intentions, presenting false sincerity. They manipulate others for personal gain, lacking honesty and transparency. This deceitful behavior erodes trust and undermines relationships. Their interactions are marked by ulterior motives, making it difficult for others to rely on or believe in them.

Appendix 5
Personal Relationship Dynamics

Finding the sweet spot in personal relationships involves striking a balance between several factors, such as communication, boundaries, mutual respect, and shared goals. This equilibrium ensures that relationships are healthy, productive, and fulfilling for all parties involved. Achieving this balance requires an understanding of the dynamics at play, self-awareness, and a commitment to continuous improvement.

Communication

Effective communication is the cornerstone of any successful relationship. It involves not just speaking but also listening actively and empathetically. In any relationship, clear communication helps in setting expectations, providing feedback, and resolving conflicts. It ensures that feelings and needs are expressed and understood. Open channels of communication prevent misunderstandings and build trust, making it easier to navigate challenges together.

Boundaries

Establishing and respecting boundaries is crucial in maintaining a healthy relationship. Boundaries define what is acceptable and what is not, preventing overreach and ensuring that each person's needs are met. In a marriage, this could mean the establishment of a clear line between work and family commitments and responsibilities. Understanding each other's limits and giving space when needed protects your well-being and prevents resentment from building up - especially in times of crisis.

Mutual Respect

Respect is the foundation of any strong relationship. It comes from valuing each other's opinions, acknowledging contributions, and treating each other with dignity. Recognizing each other's strengths and weaknesses, likes and dislikes, and working to complement each other in these areas, goes a long way to demonstrating respect for their expertise and addressing issues with fairness. Mutual respect involves appreciating each other's uniqueness, supporting each other's growth, and understanding the differences.

Shared Goals

Having aligned goals strengthens relationships by providing a common purpose. In a close friendship, it may center around a common love of sports, hobbies, church, academics, or any number of social activities. In romantic relationships or marriage, shared goals might include building a family, planning for the future, or pursuing shared hobbies. These common objectives bond people together and provide motivation to work through challenges.

Effective Collaboration

Finding the sweet spot in most relationships often involves being able to collaborate without sacrificing individual autonomy. Encourage each other to share ideas and take responsibility for their part. This not only leverages distinct abilities and passions but also promotes a sense of ownership of the outcome and shared satisfaction.

Work-Life Integration

Striking a balance between work and personal life is crucial for long-term satisfaction in marriage and family relationships. Encourage an atmosphere where everyone can manage their time effectively to provide for needs, achieve personal and mutual goals, and make memories together. For example, there is no point in making a lot of money or meeting a long-term goal yet not making any memories together – which is ultimately what family is about. Remember, a little flexibility allows for unforeseen circumstances and goes a long way to help you stay in your relational sweet spot.

Quality Time

When my boys were still in school, Monday nights were always special family nights. Junk food was consumed either in front of the television, watching a family movie, playing a fun board game, or, during the summer, taking a picnic meal out to the beach. Years later, now married and with families of their own, those Monday nights are still the topic of joyful conversation.

Quality time is about constructing your own album of mutual memories that count. Quantity does not always equate with quality. It is how you spend that time that helps strengthen bonds with loved ones and creates lasting, happy memories, ensuring that relationships remain vibrant and connected.

Independence and Togetherness

While spending time together is important, so is maintaining individuality. Encourage each other to pursue personal interests and spend a little time apart. This balance ensures that both partners grow independently while staying connected.

Shared Responsibilities

Marriage relationships are not all romance and "Hallmark Moments." There is a laundry list of more mundane things that need to get done like cleaning, maintenance, paying bills - not to mention the laundry! Sharing responsibilities prevents one person from feeling overwhelmed. Whatever the task, equitable sharing of duties reinforces a sense of partnership and fairness.

Emotional Support

Being there for each other during tough times is a cornerstone of strong personal relationships. Providing emotional support, listening without judgment, and offering encouragement, strengthens the bond and builds endurance to handle life's challenges.

Conflict Resolution

Addressing conflicts promptly and fairly is vital in maintaining a healthy relationship. Encourage a culture of openness where issues can be discussed without fear of retribution. Use conflict as an opportunity to understand different perspectives and find mutually beneficial solutions.

Conclusion

Finding the sweet spot in personal relationships is an ongoing journey that requires effort, application, and a commitment to mutual growth. By focusing on effective communication, setting clear boundaries, fostering mutual respect, and working towards shared goals, you can nurture and improve relationships that are both fulfilling and productive. Balancing independence with togetherness, providing emotional support, and continuously striving for improvement ensures that these relationships remain strong and resilient. Ultimately, the sweet spot is where both parties feel valued, understood, and motivated to support each other's growth and happiness.

"Without commitment you will never start but more importantly, without consistency you will never finish."

Denzel Washington

Actor

www.ingramcontent.com/pod-product-compliance
Lightning Source LLC
Chambersburg PA
CBHW051508120626
46551CB00012B/829